1,000+ Little Habits
of Happy, Successful
Relationships

1,000+
Little
Habits

of Happy, Successful
Relationships

MARC & ANGEL CHERNOFF

A TARCHERPERIGEE BOOK

tarcherperigee

an imprint of Penguin Random House LLC
penguinrandomhouse.com

Library of Congress Cataloging-in-Publication Data

Names: Chernoff, Marc, author. | Chernoff, Angel, author.
Title: 1000+ little habits of happy, successful relationships /
by Marc Chernoff and Angel Chernoff.
Description: New York: TarcherPerigee, Penguin Random House LLC, 2021.
Identifiers: LCCN 2020032953 (print) | LCCN 2020032954 (ebook) |
ISBN 9780593327739 (hardcover) | ISBN 9780593327746 (ebook)
Subjects: LCSH: Self-acceptance. | Families. | Interpersonal relations.
Classification: LCC BF575.S37 C44 2021 (print) | LCC BF575.S37 (ebook) |
DDC 158.2—dc23
LC record available at https://lccn.loc.gov/2020032953
LC ebook record available at https://lccn.loc.gov/2020032954

Printed in the United States of America

3rd Printing

Interior art: Fireworks, zigzag and hearts patterns by Aleksenko Julia /
Shutterstock.com; Sunburst by WANWIDesign /
Shutterstock.com

Book design by Kristin del Rosario

To all the amazing humans we've met
who have added value to our lives
and to the lives of others

Contents

Introduction

WE ARE ALL in this together—this wild world we live in—so always be kinder than necessary. What goes around comes around. No one has ever made themselves strong by showing how small someone else is. Everyone you know, love, or meet is learning something, is afraid of something, cares deeply about something, and has lost something. You know this. So keep doing your best to be extra kind today.

Be compassionate in whatever way you can. Be a beacon of hope to people you pass on the street. Embody what you know in your heart is right. And keep in mind that **many of the kindest gestures you'll ever make, and the most important things you'll ever do, won't come easy and will never be seen publicly. But they are worth doing anyway.**

Let this book be your guide—your source of daily inspiration—to stay on track in your relationships and interactions with others. Digest one page at a time with your morning coffee or your evening tea. And we promise that you won't just grow in knowledge; you'll be a person who gives back too. This book will inspire you to use what you're learning, and what you know, to make a difference. To be a blessing. To be a friend. To encourage someone. To take time to care. To let your words heal and not wound.

You have the power to improve someone else's day, perhaps even their whole life, simply by giving them your sincere presence, compassion, and kindness today. And by doing so, you have the power to transform your life too. What would it be like to open up your heart instead of closing it? What would it be like to notice your inner narratives and move through them into growth, into peace of mind and real connection? That's precisely the direction we're heading in. We're going to explore how the time you invest in creating both healthy relationships and healthy mindsets about your relationships can affect almost everything else you do in life. It's how you can truly make a difference in this world.

But before we begin, let's get one timeless lesson crystal clear: **Happiness and success in life don't start solely with your relationships. They start with your thinking and what you tell yourself today.**

In other words, the real journey of nurturing healthy relationships starts with mindful inner calmness.

ON A CHILLY evening twenty years ago, after spending nearly every waking minute with Angel for eight straight days, I knew I had to tell her just one thing. So late at night, just before she fell asleep, I whispered it in her ear. She smiled—the kind of smile that makes me smile back. And she said, "When I'm seventy-five, and I think about my life and what it was like to be young, I hope I can remember this very moment."

A few seconds later, she closed her eyes and fell asleep. The room was peaceful—almost silent. All I could hear was the soft purr of her breathing. I stayed awake thinking about the time we'd spent together and all the choices in our lives that made this moment possible. And at some point, I realized it didn't matter what we had done or where we had gone. Nor did the future hold any significance.

All that mattered was the serenity of the moment.

Just being with her, and breathing with her.

WHY DID I just share that personal story with you?

Because doing so helps remind me.

And I know you need a reminder sometimes too.

Sometimes we all need to be reminded of the beauty and sweetness of truly absorbing ourselves into the present moment—into the people, the dialogues, and the priceless little gifts that exist there.

We need to be reminded what it's like to be truly present, and accepting, and at peace.

Because too often, amid the drama and chaos of life, we forget.

We forget to simply be and breathe with those around us.

We forget to appreciate the beauty they possess, despite their flaws.

The Human Superpower of Calmness

The most fundamental aggression to ourselves and others—the most fundamental harm we can do to human nature as a whole on a daily basis—is to remain ignorant by not having the awareness or courage to look at ourselves and others honestly and gently.

All day, every day, many of us get annoyed with people and their situations when they fail to live up to our expectations, as if their reality isn't enough for us and never will be. We reject these people, as their "problems" somehow seem different from our own. We feel like we need something better, something more from them—and we scream inside!

We let our emotions and anxieties get the best of us. And we blind ourselves to the truth.

The truth is, when someone upsets us, this is often because they aren't behaving according to our fantasy of how they "should" behave. The frustration, then, stems not from their behavior but from how their behavior differs from our fantasy. Let this sink in. And let's not get carried away going forward.

Calmness is a human superpower!

Regardless of the situation, the ultimate measure of our wisdom and strength is how calm we are when facing the situation. The ability to not overreact or take things personally keeps our mind clear and our heart at peace, which instantly gives us the upper hand against the stress, fear, and confusion of the moment.

Being Calm Under Pressure

Over the past decade, we have gradually been cultivating in ourselves a new way of being—we've been taming our tendencies to get angry and irritated with people when their behavior doesn't match our expectations.

We all get frustrated when things don't play out the way we expect them to and when people don't behave like they're "supposed" to. We expect our spouses and children to act a certain way, our friends to be kind and agreeable, strangers to be less difficult, life to be easier, and so on.

And when reality hits us, and everyone and everything seems to be doing the opposite of what we want, we feel pressure inside, and then we overreact—with anger, frustration, stress, tears, etc.

So what can we do about this?

Breathe . . . and think better.

> You can't control how other people behave.
> You can't control everything that happens
> to you. What you can control is how
> you respond to it all. In your response is
> your greatest opportunity.

When you feel like your lid is about to blow, take a long, deep breath. Deep breathing releases tension, calms down our fight-or-flight reactions, and allows us to quiet our anxious nerves so that we choose more considerate and constructive responses, no matter the situation.

So, for example, do your best to inhale and exhale the next time another driver cuts you off in traffic. In a poll we conducted with our most recent Think Better, Live Better event attendees, overreacting while fighting traffic was the most commonly cited reason for overreacting on a daily basis. Just imagine if all the drivers on the road took deep breaths before making nasty hand gestures or screaming obscenities at others.

There's no doubt that it can drive us crazy when we don't get what we expect from people, especially when they are being rude and difficult. But trying to change the unchangeable, wanting others to be exactly the way we want them to be, just doesn't work. The alternative, though, is unthinkable to most of us: to breathe, to let go, to lead by example, and to accept people even when they irritate us.

Here's the way of being that we have been cultivating and advocating:

- To be truly present
- To breathe deeply and often
- To remind ourselves that we can't control other people
- To remind ourselves that other people can handle their lives however they choose
- To not take their behavior personally
- To see the good in them (even when it's hard)
- To let go of the ideals and expectations we have about others, and life in general, that cause unnecessary frustration, drama, and bouts of anger

- To remember that when others are being difficult, they are often going through a difficult time we know nothing about, and we should give them empathy, love, and space

"Being" this way takes practice, but it's worth it. It makes us less frustrated, it helps us be more mindful, it drastically improves our relationships, it lowers our stress, and it allows us to make the world a slightly more peaceful and lovable place to be.

Now it's your turn . . .

To instill a little more love into this world, even when there's no great "love story" to tell.

To love the people you are with, as much as feasibly possible, until you can be with the people who truly deserve your love.

Fewer outbursts.

Less drama.

More deep breaths, presence, and love.

Ultimately, this is the way we find calmness, peace, and new opportunities in life.

Let's practice starting today together.

This book is our guide—our daily source of practical guidance.

1,000+ Little Habits
of Happy, Successful
Relationships

PART ONE

. . . . .

Self-Love &
Self-Worth

It Starts with You

LET'S START OFF here with a hard yet vital truth: You will end up sadly disappointed in both your life and relationships if you expect people will always do for you as you do for them. Not everyone has the same heart as you have. And you don't need everyone to have a heart like yours.

While relationships can be a richly fulfilling source of intimacy, pleasure, and love, it's also true that they can trigger us to close up our hearts. This is a continuous struggle for the majority of the population, and also the single greatest point of potential for our personal growth. Which is precisely why this book—a book about happy, successful relationships—starts with "self."

When it comes to self-love, self-worth, and self-improvement, it's easy to be constantly seeking. We want more for ourselves. We want more for our families. We want more in our businesses. We want more in our careers. Being successful in these areas of life always seems to be about reaching for something. We want to attain the goal, to be one step further than we are. But to truly find a place of self-love, we need to dial it back. We need to be gentle with ourselves and take time to appreciate how far we've come, and be happy where we are right now.

One of the ways we do that is to be sure we schedule alone time when we can sit and think, perhaps by going to bed a little earlier so we can step back and take a look ahead and think about what we want to be doing with our time. This is time we put on our calendar, right next to everything we have to do for the week in the business and for our family routine, so that we can be aware of our individual needs as well as each other's needs.

We also practice self-inquiry, checking in with our own thoughts and challenging ourselves with questions like these:

- Are these thoughts true?
- Who am I with this thought in my head?
- Who would I be without this thought?
- What is the opposite of this thought, and is there any truth in that?

Angel recently started using some of her alone time to float. That's right, float. A float studio is like a spa where you can float in a pod that's filled with water and one thousand pounds of Epsom salt. It's a form of sensory deprivation that leaves you alone with your thoughts and allows for deep relaxation. Angel floats without music, and she uses it as a form of meditation. It's a way to challenge yourself to recognize thoughts and let them go without attaching to them. You want to get to the state right before you fall asleep; you may even start twitching. The idea is to be absolutely relaxed and in the present moment, without a to-do list, a destination, or any responsibilities, and to be okay with yourself as you are. Taking time for herself in this way, Angel has experienced benefits such as feeling more patient, kind, and caring toward others, and less irritable and frustrated.

All of these self-love and self-worth practices ultimately mean we take care of ourselves so that we can bring our best self into our relationships—with each other; with our son, Mac, and the rest of our family, and with our friends. If you want to improve your relationships, the first place to start is always with yourself.

3 Little Reminders
That Will Make You Feel
Way Less Alone

IN THE MIDST of bad days and hard times, it's easy to look around and see a bunch of people who seem to be doing perfectly fine. Things are not as perfect as they seem. We're all struggling in our own unique way, every single day. And if we could just be brave enough to open up about it, and talk to each other more often, we'd realize that we are not alone in feeling lost and alone with our issues.

So many of us are fighting a similar battle right now. Try to remember this. No matter how embarrassed or uneasy you feel about your own situation, others are out there experiencing the same emotions. When you hear yourself say, "I am all alone," it's just your troubled subconscious mind trying to sell you a lie.

There's always someone who can relate to you.

There's always someone who understands.

Perhaps you can't immediately talk to them, but they are out there. We are out there.

The whole reason we wrote these words is because we often feel and think and struggle much like you do. We care about many of the things you care about, just in our own way. And although some people do not understand us, we understand each other.

You are definitely not alone!

We are not alone!

And to further assure you of this, let us tell you a quick story about a strong and beautiful woman we know who has recently felt alone too.

What She Desires Most

She notices the people sitting in a small sports bar across the street. They're cheering and chatting. They look so alive. She wants to cross the street to join these people, just to connect with them—to be a part of something. But a subtle voice that comes from within, that whispers from the open wounds in her heart, holds her back from doing so. So she keeps walking. Alone.

She walks to the end of the city center, where she sees a dirt path that leads up a grassy hill. The hill, she knows, overlooks a spiritual sanctuary. But it isn't the sanctuary she wants to visit tonight—not yet anyway. It's a warm, breezy Saturday night, and she wants to find a place outdoors with sufficient light so that she can sit and read the book she's grasping in her right hand.

But reading isn't what she really wants. Not deep down. What she really wants is for someone—anyone at all—to tap her on the shoulder and invite her into their world. To ask her questions and tell her stories. To be interested. To understand her. To laugh with her. To want her to be a part of their life.

At the deepest level, in the core of her soul, what she desires most is to know that she's not alone in the world. That she truly belongs. And that whatever she was put here to do, in time it will be done and shared with others who deeply care.

An Unsustainable Past

This young woman left a substantial segment of her life behind to be in this small city tonight. A few months earlier, she was engaged to a strapping young businessman, with whom she owned a fast-growing start-up company, working long, hard days and enjoying the fruits of their labor together with a deepening community of friendships in Manhattan.

In a period of just a few months, she and her fiancé split up and decided that it was easiest to shut down the company and divide the monetary remains rather than attempt co-ownership. As they began the process of shutting down the company, she learned that most of the seemingly deep friendships she had made in Manhattan were tied directly to her old business affairs or her business-socialite of an ex-fiancé.

While this young woman didn't consciously expect such a rapid and painful series of events, it also wasn't totally unexpected. Subconsciously she knew that she had created a life for herself that was unsustainable. It was a life centered on her social status, in which all her relationships brought with them a mounting and revolving set of expectations. This life left no time for spiritual growth or deep connection or love.

Yet this young woman is drawn to spirituality, connection, and love. She has been drawn to these things all her life. And the only thing that steered her off course into this unsustainable lifestyle was the careless belief that if she did certain things and acted in certain ways, she would be worthy in the eyes of others. That her social status would procure lasting admiration from others. And that she would never feel alone.

She realizes now how wrong she was.

The Sanctuary

The young woman walks up a steep paved road on the outskirts of the city center. She feels the burn in her calf muscles as she marches higher and higher. The road is, at first, filled with quaint boutiques and young couples and friends, but as it advances uphill, they give way to small cottage homes and kids playing with flashlights in the street. She keeps marching higher and higher until she reaches a clearing where there is a small public park.

In this park, a group of teenagers are huddled around two guitarists, who are strumming and singing an acoustic melody. "Is it a popular song?" she thinks to herself. She isn't sure because she hasn't had time lately to listen to music. She wants to join the group. She wants to tell the guitarists that their music is incredible. But she hesitates. She just can't find the nerve to walk over to them.

Instead, she sits on a park bench a few hundred feet away. The bench overlooks the cityscape below. She stares off into the distance and up into the night sky for several minutes, thinking and breathing. And she begins to smile, because she can see the spiritual sanctuary. It's dark outside, but the sanctuary shines bright. She can see it clearly. She can feel its warmth surrounding her. And although she knows the sanctuary has existed for an eternity, her heart tells her something that stretches a smile across her cheeks: "This sanctuary is all yours tonight."

Not in the sense that she owns it. Nor in the sense that it isn't also a sanctuary for millions of other people around the world. But rather in the sense that it belongs to all of us as part of our heritage, exclusively tailored for every human being and our unique needs and beliefs. It's a quiet refuge that, when we choose to pay attention, exists all around us and within us. We can escape to it at any time. It's a place where we can

dwell with the good spirits and guardian angels who love us uncondi-
tionally and guide us even when we feel lost and alone.

Especially when we feel lost and alone.

Reminders for When *You* Feel Lost & Alone

We hope this short story makes you feel less alone. We hope it gives you
hope. But assuming you need a little extra perspective right now—
because sometimes we all do—we want to shift gears and cover a few
practical reminders we often examine with our course students:

1. Every passing face on the street represents a story every bit as captivating, complicated, and crazy as yours.

Remember that everyone has a story. Everyone has gone through something that's unexpectedly changed them and forced them to grow. Everyone you meet has struggled, and continues to struggle in some way,
and to them, it's just as hard as what you're going through.

Marc was lucky enough to have a very wise grandmother who
coached him through this reality when he was just a teenager. And he
was smart enough to write a journal entry about the conversation he
had with her, so he could remember her wisdom decades later. Here's a
little taste of that conversation from Marc's journal:

> I sat there in her living room staring at her through teary
> eyes. "I feel lost and alone and completely out of my mind," I
> said. "I don't know what's wrong with me."
>
> "Why do you feel that way?" she delicately asked.
>
> "Because I'm neurotic and self-conscious and regretful,
> and so much more all at once," I said.
>
> "And you don't think everyone feels the way you do some-
> times?" she asked.

"Not like this!" I proclaimed.

"Well, honey, you're wrong," she said. "If you think you know someone who never feels the way you do right now—who never feels a bit lost and alone, and downright confused and crazy—you just don't know enough about them. Every one of us contains a measure of 'crazy' that moves us in strange, often perplexing ways. This side of us is necessary; it's part of our human ability to think, adapt, and grow. It's part of being intelligent," she said. "No great mind has ever existed without a touch of this kind of madness."

I sat silently for a moment. My eyes gazed from her eyes to the ground and back to her eyes again. "So you're saying I should want to feel like this?"

"To an extent," she said. "Let me put it this way: Taking all your feelings seriously all the time, and letting them drive you into misery, is a waste of your incredible spirit. You alone get to choose what matters and what doesn't. The meaning of everything in your life is the meaning you give it."

"I guess," I replied under my breath.

She continued, "And sometimes how you feel simply won't align with how you want to feel—it's mostly just your subconscious mind's way of helping you look at things from a different perspective. These feelings will come and go quickly as long as you let them go . . . as long as you consciously acknowledge them and then push through them. At least that's what I've learned to do for myself, out of necessity, on a very regular basis. So you and I are actually struggling through this one together, honey. And I'm also pretty certain we're not the only ones."

We shared another moment of silence, then my lips curled up slightly, and I cracked a smile. "Thank you, Grandma," I said.

2. You are far more than that one broken piece of you.

When times are tough, and some piece of you is chipped and broken, it's easy to feel like everything—*all* of you—is broken along with it. But that's not true.

We all have this picture in our minds of ourselves—this idea of what kind of person we are. When this idea gets even slightly harmed or threatened, we react defensively and oftentimes irrationally. People may question whether we did a good job, and this threatens our idea of being a competent person, so we become angry or hurt by the criticism. Someone falsely accuses us of something and this damages our idea that we're a good person, and so we get angry and attack the other person, or we cower and cry. And the list goes on.

But the craziest thing is, oftentimes we are actually the ones harming and threatening ourselves with negativity and false-accusations.

Just this morning, Marc was struggling to motivate himself to work on a new creative project he'd been procrastinating doing. So his identity of himself as someone who is always productive and motivated and has great ideas suddenly came under attack. When he realized he wasn't getting things done, it made him feel terribly self-conscious and uncertain, because he began subconsciously worrying that he wasn't who he thought he was. And this, in turn, made him feel very alone inside.

His solution was to realize that he's not just one thing. He's not always productive—sometimes he is, but sometimes he's unproductive too. He's not always motivated—sometimes he is, but other times he can be a bit lazy or simply in need of some downtime. And obviously he doesn't always have great ideas either—because that's impossible.

The truth is, each of us can be many things, and remembering this helps us stretch our identity so it's not so fragile—so it doesn't completely shatter when a small piece of it gets chipped. Then it doesn't matter if someone occasionally thinks we didn't do a good job, or if we sometimes catch ourselves not doing a good job—because we've already accepted that, like everyone else, we're only human.

We make mistakes.

We are less than perfect.

Just like *you*.

And that's perfectly okay.

3. There are people in this world who desperately need your support right now.

We all have the tendency to put ourselves at the center of the universe and to see everything from the viewpoint of how it affects us. But this can have all kinds of adverse effects, from feeling sorry for ourselves when things aren't going exactly as planned, to doubting ourselves when we aren't perfect, to feeling lost and alone with our issues when we're having a bad day or going through hard times.

So whenever we catch ourselves lingering at the center in an adverse state of mind, we do our best to briefly shift our focus away from our own issues and onto other people around us that we might be able to help. Finding little ways to help others gets us out of self-centered thinking, and then we're not wallowing alone in self-pity anymore—we start to think about what others need. We're not doubting ourselves, because the question of whether we are good enough is no longer the central question. The central question now is about what others need.

Thus, thinking about others instead of oneself helps solve feelings of self-consciousness and inadequacy, which in turn makes you feel a lot less broken and alone when you're struggling.

It's one of life's great paradoxes: When we serve others, we end up benefiting as much as, if not more than, those we serve. So whenever you feel a bit lost and alone with your own issues, try to shift your focus from your circumstances to the circumstances of those around you. Instead of asking, "What's wrong with me?" ask, "How can I help you?" Find someone who could use an extra hand and make a small, reasonable offer they can't refuse. The perspective you gain from doing so will guide you forward.

Closing Thoughts . . . on Being Alone

We'd like to end this discussion by directly addressing fellow souls out there who are tired and weary and struggling to find happiness at this very moment, seemingly alone.

We know you're reading this. And we want you to know we are writing this for *you*. Others will be confused. They will think we are writing this for them. But we're not.

This one's for *you*.

We want you to know that we understand. Life is not always easy. Every day can be an unpredictable challenge. Some days it can be difficult just to get out of bed in the morning, to face reality and put on that smile. But we want you to know that your smile has kept both of us going on more days than we can count. Never forget that even when times get tough, as they sometimes will, you are incredible—you really are.

So please try to smile more often. Even when times are hard, you have so many reasons to. Time and time again, our reason is you.

You won't always be perfect, and neither will we. Because nobody is perfect, and nobody deserves to be perfect. Everybody has issues. Nobody has it easy. You will never know exactly what we're going through, and we will never know exactly what you're going through. We are all fighting our own unique war.

But we are fighting through it simultaneously, together.

If someone discredits you and tells you that you can't do something, keep in mind that they are speaking from within the boundaries of their own limitations. In this crazy world that's trying to make you the same as everyone else, find the courage to keep being your awesome self. And when they laugh at you for being different, go ahead and smile back at them with confidence.

Remember, our courage doesn't always roar aloud. Sometimes it's the quiet voice at the end of the day whispering, "I will try again tomorrow." So stand strong. Things turn out best for people who make the best out of the way things turn out.

12 Ways to Stop Worrying About What Everyone Thinks of You

"WHAT'S WRONG WITH wanting others to like you?"

We frequently get emails asking us this question. Seeking approval from others is perfectly fine up until the point where you are compromising your health and happiness in the process. It becomes a serious problem if you feel as though widespread positive approval from others is the very oxygen you need to breathe. There was a time in Marc's life when he felt exactly this way.

He literally felt short of breath—almost as if he'd die—if his peers didn't approve of him. This is a condition that developed when he was very young, after kids in grade school teased him for being a nerd. He did everything he could to win their approval. And although he grew out of that awkward stage pretty early in his teenage years, the damage was done—he was left feeling insecure. He was conditioned to seek and beg for outside approval at all times.

The big problem was that, as a twentysomething college graduate entering the workforce, Marc felt that anything he did or even thought had validity only if it was the "right thing" to say and think. And by "right thing," he really meant "what other people thought was right." Marc was terrified to step outside the box of what was acceptable—which was especially harmful to his creativity as he tried to nurture his passion for writing and blogging.

Once Marc realized what he was doing, he read several books, spoke with a coach, and focused diligently on healing this broken part of himself.

It's an important lesson to learn that tying your self-worth to everyone else's opinions gives you a flawed sense of reality. But before we look at how to fix this, we first need to understand why we do this.

From wanting others to think we're attractive to checking the number of likes and comments on our Facebook and Instagram posts, most of us care about what others think. In fact, a big part of this is an innate desire: It has been proved time and time again that babies' emotions are often drawn directly from the behaviors of those around them.

As we grow up, we learn to separate our thoughts and emotions from everyone else's, but many of us continue to seek—and in many cases beg for—positive social validation from others. This can cause serious trouble when it comes to self-esteem and happiness. In a recent survey we did with three thousand of our course members and coaching clients, 67 percent of them admitted that their self-worth is strongly tied to what other people think of them.

Over a century ago, the social psychologist Charles Cooley identified the phenomenon of the "looking-glass self," which is when we believe "I am not what I think I am, and I am not what you think I am—I am what I think that you think I am." This kind of external validation has insecurity at its core, and relying on it for even a short time chips away at our sense of self-worth and self-confidence.

The biggest problem is, we tend to forget that people judge us based on a pool of influences in their own lives that have absolutely nothing to do with us, including their own past experiences, biases, and looking-glass selves. Basing your self-worth on what others think puts you in a perpetual state of vulnerability—you are literally at the mercy of their unreliable perspectives. If they see you in the right light, and respond to you in a positive, affirming manner, then you feel good about yourself. And if not, you feel like you did something wrong.

Bottom line: When you're doing everything for other people, and basing your happiness and self-worth on their opinions, you've lost the core of who you are. Constant approval-seeking forces you to miss out on the beauty of simply being yourself, with your own unique ideas and desires. If you are led through life only doing and being what you've come to believe is expected of you, then, in a way, you cease to live. The good news is we have the capacity to watch our thoughts and expectations, identify what ones serve us, and then change the ones that do not. And once you do so, your relationships will have an increased potential to be far deeper and more authentic.

So how can you stop fearing what everyone thinks of you? How can you settle in to the core of who you are? Let's take a look:

First, we must understand that the vast majority of our fears and anxieties amount to one thing: loss.

We fear

- Losing our youth
- Losing our social status
- Losing our money
- Losing control
- Losing our comfort
- Losing our life

We also fear, perhaps more than anything else, being rejected by others. This kind of fear is widespread and debilitating if left unaddressed. Why is this fear so deeply entrenched in us? In ancient tribal times, being rejected from the safety of the community could have meant death. So it's no wonder, really, that we want to be accepted by others.

Fear is an instinctual human emotion designed to keep us aware and safe—like the headlights on a car clearly illuminating the twists and turns on the road ahead. But too much fear, like high beams blinding us on a dark, foggy road, can cause the loss of the very thing we feared losing in the first place.

This is especially true when it comes to the fear of rejection. Here's another example from Marc's life:

When he was a teenager, Marc was always the outcast trying desperately to fit in with his peers. He bounced around to three different schools, and various social circles in each school, within a four-year span, and he faced rejection after rejection. Marc distinctly remembers shooting hoops on the basketball court by himself on numerous occasions, always the new kid, always longing for acceptance. For the longest time, Marc thought these childhood-outcast experiences were the root cause of his obsessive, people-pleasing ways in adulthood.

Do you look for acceptance and reassurance from others too?

If so, you now know you're not alone. And what we have learned over the years is this: Constantly seeking acceptance and reassurance from other people is a dead-end journey. These things can be found only within you, not from others. Because any look, word, or reaction from someone else can be warped and misinterpreted.

So in order to stop worrying so much about what others think, it's time to inject some fresh objectivity into your life, and develop a value system that doesn't depend on others every step of the way. Here are twelve things you can start doing today:

1. Realize that fear itself is the real problem.

Franklin D. Roosevelt so profoundly said, "The only thing we have to fear is fear itself." Nothing could be closer to the truth. This is especially true as it relates to self-fulfilling prophecies.

A self-fulfilling prophecy is a false belief about a situation that motivates the person with the belief to take actions that cause the belief to come true. This kind of thinking often kills opportunities and tears relationships apart. For instance, you might wrongly believe that a group of people will reject you, so you become defensive and anxious, and perhaps even hostile with them. Eventually, your behavior brings about the feared rejection, which wasn't there to begin with. And then you, "the prophet," feel that you were right from the very beginning: "I knew they didn't like me!"

Do you see how this works? Look carefully at your own tendencies. How do your fears and beliefs about possible rejection influence your behavior toward others? Take a stand. Instead of letting fear show you what might be wrong in your relationships, start looking for signs of what might be right.

2. Let go of your "end of the world" thinking.

All variations of fear, including the fear of rejection, thrive on "end of the world" thinking. In other words, our emotions convince us that an undesirable outcome results in annihilation.

- What if they don't like me?
- What if he rejects me?
- What if I don't fit in, and I'm left sitting alone at the party?

None of these things result in the end of the world, but if we convince ourselves that they do, we will irrationally fear these outcomes and give our fears control over us. The truth is, we human beings are inefficient at accurately predicting how future misfortune will make us feel. In fact, most of the time we avoid consciously thinking about it altogether, which only perpetuates our subconscious fears.

So ask yourself, "If disaster should strike, and my fear of being rejected comes true, what are three constructive ways I could cope and move forward with my life?" Sit down and tell yourself a story (write it down too if it helps) about how you will feel after rejection, how you will allow yourself to be upset for a short while, and then how you will begin the process of growing from the experience and moving on. Just doing this exercise will help you feel less fear around the possibility of rejection.

What other people think of you really doesn't matter that much.

3. Question what "rejection" really means.

If a person discovers a 200-karat white diamond in the earth but, due to ignorance, believes it to be worthless, and thus tosses it aside, does this tell us more about the diamond or the person? Along the same lines, when one person rejects another, it reveals a lot more about the *rejecter* than the *rejected*. All you are really seeing is the often shortsighted opinion of one person. Consider the following:

If J. K. Rowling stopped writing after being rejected by multiple publishers for years, there would be no Harry Potter. If Howard Schultz gave up after being turned down by banks two hundred times, there would be no Starbucks. If Walt Disney quit too soon after his theme park concept was trashed by three hundred investors, there would be no Disney World.

One thing is for sure: If you give too much power to the opinions of others, you will become their prisoner. So never let someone's opinion alter your reality. Never sacrifice who you are, or who you aspire to be, just because someone else has a problem with it. Love who you are inside and out, and keep pushing forward. No one has the power to make you feel small unless you give them that power. And when someone rejects you, don't assume it's because you're unworthy or unlovable. Because in many ways, all they've really done is give you feedback about their own shortsightedness.

4. Be fully present and aware of how you *do* want to feel.

Ever noticed how people who are struggling with emotional challenges tend to tell you how they don't want to feel? Fair enough, but at some point we all need to focus on how we *do* want to feel.

When you're in a social situation that's making you anxious, forget what you don't want to feel for a moment. Work out how you *do* want to feel right now in the present moment. Train yourself to live right here, right now, without regretting how others once made you feel or fearing the possibility of future judgment.

This is *your* choice. You *can* change the way you think.

If you were administering lifesaving mouth-to-mouth resuscitation in public, you'd be 100 percent focused and present. You wouldn't be thinking about what bystanders thought of your hair, your body type, or the brand of jeans you were wearing. All these inconsequential details would vanish from your consciousness. The intensity of the situation would banish from your mind any care about what others might be thinking of you. This illustrates, quite simply, that thinking about what others are thinking about you is *your choice*.

5. Let go of your need to be right.

The reason your fear of rejection sometimes gets the best of you is because a part of you believes you're always right. If you think someone doesn't like you, then surely they don't. Right? *Wrong!*

People who never question their emotions, especially when they're feeling sad or anxious, make life much more difficult than it has to be. It's time to let go a little. Being more confident in life partly means being okay with not knowing what's going to happen, so you can relax and allow things to play out naturally. Relaxing with not knowing is the key to confidence in relationships and peace in life.

So here's a new mantra for you—say it, and then say it again: "This is my life, my choices, my mistakes, and my lessons. I have nothing to prove. And as long as I'm not hurting people, I need not worry what they think of me."

6. Embrace and enjoy your individuality.

Constantly seeking approval means we're perpetually worried that others are forming negative judgments of us. This steals the fun, ingenuity, and spontaneity from our lives. Flip the switch on this habit.

It takes a lot of courage to stand alone, but it's worth it. Being unapologetically *you* is worth it! Your real friends in life will reveal themselves slowly—they're the ones who truly know you and love you just the same.

Bottom line: Don't change so that people will like you; be yourself and the right people will love the real you.

7. Remind yourself that most people are *not* thinking about you anyway.

Ethel Barrett once said, "We would worry far less about what others think of us if we realized how seldom they do." Nothing could be closer to the truth.

Forget what everyone else thinks of you today; chances are, they aren't thinking about you anyway. If you feel like they always are, understand that this perception of them watching you and critiquing your every move is a complete figment of your imagination. It's your own inner fears and insecurities that are creating this illusion.

It's you judging yourself that's the real problem.

8. Acknowledge that external validation is only getting in your way.

Spend time clearly and consciously articulating to yourself how your thoughts about what others are (potentially) thinking play out in your life. Think of situations where these thoughts get in your way, and identify the triggers and the regrettable responses they cause in your life. Then identify a new behavior that creates a more beneficial response.

Tell yourself, "Instead of responding in the same old way based on what I think others are thinking, I will respond in this new way based on my new way of thinking about myself." Every time you interrupt your automatic response and respond differently, you are rewiring your brain to think more effectively.

The ultimate goal is to never let someone's opinion become your reality. To never sacrifice who you are, or who you aspire to be, because someone else has a problem with it. And to realize once and for all that no one else has the power to make you feel small unless you give them that power.

9. Get comfortable with not knowing what other people think.

When we first started writing our blog, we'd agonize over whether people would think what we wrote was good enough. We desperately hoped they'd like it, and oftentimes we'd catch ourselves imagining they didn't. Then one day we realized how much energy we were wasting worrying about it. So we've gradually learned to relax with simply not knowing.

Some problems in life, such as not knowing what others think of you, are not really meant to be resolved. As we've mentioned, how people perceive you may have more to do with them than with you anyway. They may even like or dislike you simply because you've triggered an association in their minds by reminding them of someone they liked or disliked from their past, which has absolutely nothing to do with you.

10. Refocus your attention on what *does* matter.

People will think what they want to think. You can't control them. No matter how carefully you choose your words and mannerisms, there's always a good chance they'll be misinterpreted and twisted upside down by someone. Does this really matter in the grand scheme of things? No, it doesn't.

What *does* matter is how you see yourself.

So when you're making big decisions, make a habit of staying 100 percent true to your values and convictions. Never be ashamed of doing what feels right.

To help you implement this positive habit, start by listing out five to ten things that are important to you when it comes to building your character and living your life honorably. For example:

- Honesty
- Reliability
- Self-respect
- Self-discipline
- Compassion
- Progression
- Positivity

Having a list like this to reference will give you an opportunity to consciously invoke your handpicked traits/behaviors in place of doing something random simply for the purpose of external validation. While it may sound overly simplistic, most people never take the time to actually decide what is important to them when it comes to their self-image—they let others decide for them.

11. Accept that someone else's opinion is *not* your problem.

How many times have you looked at a person and initially misjudged their brilliance? Appearances are deceptive. How you seem to someone and how you actually are, are rarely congruent. Even if they get the basic gist of who you are, they're still missing a big piece of the puzzle. What someone thinks of you will rarely contain the whole truth, which is fine.

If someone forms an opinion of you based on superficialities, then it's up to them, not you, to reform those opinions based on a more objective and rational viewpoint. Leave it to them to worry about—that is, if they even have an opinion at all.

Bottom line: Other people's opinions of you are their problem, not yours. The less you worry about what they think of you, the less complicated your life becomes.

12. Speak and live your truth.

Speak your truth even if your voice shakes. Be cordial and reasonable, of course, but don't tread carefully on every word you say. Push your concerns of what others might think aside. Let the consequences of doing so unravel naturally. What you'll find is that most of the time no one will be offended or irritated at all. And if they do get upset, it's likely only because you've started behaving in a way that challenges their limited perspective.

Think about it. Why be fake?

In the end, the truth usually comes out one way or the other, and when that happens, you're standing alone if you've been holding yourself back. So live your whole truth starting now. If someone gives you a hard time and says, "You've changed," it's not a bad thing. It just means you stopped living your life their way. Don't apologize for it. Instead, be open and sincere, explain how you feel, and keep doing what you know in your heart is right.

Afterthoughts

You don't need a standing ovation or a bestseller or a promotion or a million bucks. You have nothing to prove. You are enough right now. Go ahead and meditate on that for a minute . . .

You are enough right now.

Care less about who you are to others and more about who you are to yourself. You will have fewer heartaches and disappointments the minute you stop seeking from others the validation only *you* can give yourself.

A life spent ceaselessly trying to please people, who perhaps are incapable of even being pleased, or trying too hard to always be seen as doing "the right thing," is a sure road to a regretful existence.

Do more than just exist. We all exist. The question is: Do you live?

20 Things to Remember When Rejection Hurts

AS YOU LOOK back on your life, you will realize that many of the times you thought you were being rejected by someone or from something you wanted, you were in fact being redirected to someone or something you needed.

Seeing this when you're in the midst of feeling rejected, however, is quite tough. As soon as someone critiques, criticizes, and pushes you away—as soon as you are rejected—you find yourself thinking, "Well, that proves once again that I'm not worthy." What you need to realize is, the other person or situation is *not* worthy of *you* and your particular journey.

Rejection is necessary medicine; it teaches you how to turn away from relationships and opportunities that aren't going to work so that you can find the right ones that will. It doesn't mean you aren't good enough; it just means someone else failed to notice what you have to offer. Which means you now have more time to improve yourself and explore your options.

Will you be bitter for a moment? Absolutely. Hurt? Of course—you're human. There isn't a soul on this planet who doesn't feel a small fraction of their heart break at the realization of rejection. For a short time afterward, you will ask yourself every question you can think of:

- What did I do wrong?
- Why didn't they care about me?
- How come?

But then you have to let your emotions fuel you in a positive way! This is the important part. Let your feelings of rejection drive you, feed you, and inspire one heck of a powerful opening to the next chapter of your story.

Honestly, if you constantly feel like someone is not treating you with respect, check your price tag. Perhaps you've subconsciously marked yourself down. Because it's *you* who tells others what you're worth by showing them what you're willing to accept for your time and attention. So get off the clearance rack. And we mean right *now*! If you don't value and respect yourself, wholeheartedly, no one else will either.

We know it's hard to accept, but think about it . . .

All too often we let the rejections of our past dictate every move we make thereafter. We literally do not know ourselves to be any better than what some intolerant person or shallow circumstance once told us was true. It's time to realize this and squash the subconscious idea that you don't deserve any better. It's time to remind yourself that . . .

1. The person you liked, loved, or respected in the past, who treated you like dirt again and again, has nothing intellectually or spiritually to offer you in the present moment but headaches and heartache.

2. One of the most rewarding and important moments in life is when you finally find the courage to let go of what you can't change, like someone else's behavior or decisions.

3. Life and God both have greater plans for you that don't involve crying at night or believing that you're broken.

4. The harsh truth is, sometimes you have to get knocked down lower than you have ever been to stand up taller and emotionally stronger than you ever were before.

5. It's not the end of the world—it's never the end of the world—and yet rejection can make the loss of someone or something you weren't even that crazy about feel gut-wrenching and world-ending.

6. Sometimes people don't notice the things we do for them until we stop doing them. And sometimes the more chances you give, the more respect you lose. Enough is enough. Never let a person get comfortable with disrespecting you. You deserve better. You deserve to be with someone who makes you smile, someone who doesn't take you for granted, someone who won't leave you hanging.

7. Some chapters in our lives have to close without closure. There's no point in losing yourself by trying to fix what's meant to stay broken.

8. Take a deep breath. Inner peace begins the moment you decide not to let another person or event control your emotions.

9. You really can't take things other people say about you too personally. What they think and say is a reflection of them, not of you.

10. Those with the strength to succeed in the long run are the ones who build themselves up with the bricks others have thrown at them.

11. Let your scars remind you that the damage someone has inflicted on you has left you stronger, smarter, and more resilient.

12. When you lose someone or something, don't think of it as a loss, but as a gift that lightens your load so that you can better travel the path meant for you.

13. You will never miss out on what is meant for you, even if it has to come to you in a roundabout way. Stay focused. Be positive.

14. Rejections and naysayers aren't that important in the grand scheme of things; so don't let them conquer your mind. Step forward! Seriously, most of us do not understand how much potential we have—we limit our aspirations to the level someone else told us was possible.

15. Too many people overvalue what they are not and undervalue what they are. Don't be one of them. Ultimately, you are who you are when nobody's watching. Know this! And dare to be yourself, however awkward, different, or odd that self may prove to be to someone else.

16. Comparing yourself with others, or other people's perceptions, only undermines your worth, your education, and your own inner wisdom. No one can handle your present situation better than *you*.

17. The more we fill our lives with genuine passion and purpose, the less time and energy we waste looking for approval from everyone else.

18. You *can* use your struggles, frustrations, and rejections to motivate you rather than annoy you. You are in control of the way you look at life.

19. Sometimes transitions in life mean something even better is coming your way, so embrace them and don't be afraid to let go.

20. Right now is a new beginning. The possibilities ahead are endless. Be strong enough to let go, wise enough to move forward, diligent enough to work hard, and patient enough to wait for what you deserve.

Afterthoughts

All details aside, you don't need anyone's constant affection or approval in order to be good enough in this world. When someone rejects or abandons or judges you, it isn't actually about you. It's about them and their own insecurities, limitations, and needs. So you don't have to internalize any of it! Your worth isn't contingent on other people's acceptance of you. You're allowed to be yourself. You're allowed to voice your thoughts and feelings. You're allowed to assert your needs. You're allowed to hold on to the truth that who you are is more than enough. And you're allowed to let go of anyone in your life who makes you feel otherwise.

8 Ways to Be Emotionally Strong in Your Relationships

MARC IS THE first to admit that he used to be emotionally weak in relationships—not in a silly, desperate way, but in the same way that many of us are. He wanted somebody to make him happy, blamed others for his sadness, and sought to fulfill his emotional needs through other people's constant validation.

This behavior created three distinct emotional difficulties for Marc:

- He had a lot of relationship problems, because if the other person's behavior wasn't satisfying his needs, he'd get upset and resent it.
- He was often unhappy, because he was looking for happiness outside of himself, expecting others to somehow fill his self-love deficit.
- He felt helpless and stuck in many cases, because if other people are supposed to fulfill our needs and make us happy, then what happens when they don't? What could he do if they decided to hurt him instead?

Fast-forward to today, and it's clear that Marc has spent the better part of the past two decades turning things around and cultivating his emotional strength. And it has made a world of difference—his relationships are healthier (including our marriage!), and he's happier.

When we began our blog and our coaching practice several years ago, countless people who were suffering from the same kinds of emotional weaknesses Marc used to have started coming to us. So we began sharing the strategies that helped him heal, and not surprisingly, they worked for these people too. We've refined them gradually over the years into a very useful, simple process.

The first step . . .

Test Your Emotional Strength

Are you emotionally weak and dependent on others for your happiness? Ask yourself these simple questions:

- Are you looking for a partner to make you happy?
- If you're in an intimate relationship, do you look to this person to validate all your needs?
- When you're alone, do you feel pressure to fill your time with constant distraction? Are you always on your phone/tablet/computer/ etc. when you're alone?
- Do you get upset if your partner doesn't do things your way?
- Is your relationship your entire world? What about your relationships with friends or other family remembers? Can you tell where their needs end and yours begin?
- Do you get upset if your partner doesn't include you in what they're doing 24/7?
- Do you struggle with jealousy?

Obviously, this list isn't comprehensive, but we're willing to bet you can see yourself in a couple of those questions, at least to a certain degree.

And that doesn't mean you're broken. Most people struggle with several of these issues, though many will likely deny it because they'll worry it might make them look inferior to others. No one likes to look that way or to think of themselves as weak. But dealing with any of these issues makes you human—it simply means you have something positive to work on.

How We Become Emotionally Weak in Our Relationships

The kind of thinking that leads to emotional weakness typically starts in childhood. We rely on our parents for all our emotional needs—love, comfort, validation, and so on. And when we lean on them too much, often we don't fully develop the skills to independently support our emotional strength as children, because our parents, out of love, do their best to provide for all our needs.

Then we grow into adulthood without having learned how to stand strong on our own. So we look for someone else to hold us up and fill our emotional needs. We look for the perfect partner, and will likely go through several breakups because . . .

1. We are not emotionally independent, and so we do "needy" things that hurt our relationships.

2. Our partners are struggling in the same way.

If we're ever hurt, we blame the other person for hurting us. If they aren't there for us when we need them, we blame them some more. If they treat us poorly again and again, we become victims, because we can't possibly move on with our lives if someone has done something cruel to us, right? Wrong. If you can relate to any of this, there is a solution, and it requires you to look within for the happiness and validation you seek. But first, let us give you a few important points to think about:

What You Must Remember

- If your happiness is dependent only on the acceptance and approval of other people, then *you* are giving away far too much of your power. It's human nature to want to be liked and admired, to want to be included, but it's damaging for your self-esteem and emotional strength if it's something you have to constantly fight for.

- At the end of the day, how confident you are is essential to the results you will see from your efforts (especially in your relationships). And on a deeper level, when you know you can count on yourself to do the things you say you want to do, it becomes easier to believe that you'll be successful at bigger, riskier things. Remember that practice makes progress in all areas of your life.

- Happiness is something you decide on, on your own, in the present moment. Whether you like your home or not doesn't depend on how the furniture is arranged; it's how you arrange your mind. You have to decide to love it just the way it is. It's a decision you make every morning when you wake up—you can spend the day in bed recounting the problems with the parts of your life that no longer exist, or you can get out of bed and be thankful for the parts that do exist. It's up to you, and only you.

- All the validation you need is yours to give yourself. So the next time you feel pressured to impress someone, try taking a deep breath and reminding yourself that you don't owe anyone your justification. Revel in the reality that you get to choose. You have the authority to decide how to spend your time and energy. And here's the real beauty of it: When you don't owe anyone anything, you're free to give and love from the heart.

- When you change how you show up to life, everything in your life changes. That's the powerful part of the simple steps below. By becoming emotionally stronger, you have the power to change not only your world but other people's worlds as well. You have the power to change the entire world in some small way by showing up as the strongest version of yourself. The present and future are not set in stone—they are in your hands.

Becoming Emotionally Strong

At this point it should be clear that other people are an unreliable source for meeting your own emotional needs—they will come and go, or they'll be emotionally unavailable sometimes for their own personal, uncontrollable reasons.

The good news is, your emotional strength (happiness, validation, and so on) doesn't require their involvement. It is within you, always. How can you find it and tap into it? It takes some inner searching, and lots of practice, but consider these simple strategies we've seen work wonders in hundreds of people's lives over the years:

1. Sit by yourself for twenty minutes each day, without a phone, tablet, TV, or other distraction. Look inside—meditate. Notice your thoughts as they come up. Get to know your mind. See how fascinating it is as you jump from one thought to the next. This in itself is an infinite source of entertainment and learning.

2. Create something. Come up with ideas for building something from the ground up and then do it: a poem, a painting, a song, an action plan,

a business. You don't need anyone to do those things, and they give you added insight into your own abilities and passions.

3. Exercise your curiosity, a boundless source of happiness for most people. Explore. Travel. Educate yourself. Read good books. Deepen your knowledge base on topics you enjoy.

4. Talk yourself through your own problems. Find a solution. If you're bored, fix it. If you are lonely or hurt, comfort yourself. If you're jealous, don't hope that someone will reassure you; reassure yourself.

5. Take responsibility. If you find yourself blaming others, tell yourself that the other person is never the problem. Of course, you can choose to believe the other person is the problem, but then you are dependent on them for a solution. If you believe that they aren't the problem, then you are able to look inside yourself for the solution.

6. Stop complaining, and instead find a way to be grateful.

7. Don't indulge yourself in being needy, but instead find a way to give.

8. Give up on waiting for someone to help you and instead help yourself.

As you can tell, these strategies don't really have anything to do with your relationships, at least not directly. They are about *you* becoming an emotionally strong individual who enters all future relationships, or reenters present ones, with a newfound inner strength. You create your own source of built-in happiness and validation, and then you walk around as a whole, happy human being, needing nothing more.

Come from this place of wholeness, of emotional strength and independence, and then love others. Not because you need them to love you back, not because you're desperate to be needed, but because loving them is a miraculous thing to do.

5 Ways to Stop Feeling Insecure in Your Relationships

A GOOD RELATIONSHIP is about sharing ideas and enjoyable moments with another, helping each other grow in healthy ways, both together socially and as individuals. If someone really does treat you poorly or lies and cheats you out of something, feeling insecure is a natural and reasonable response. However, if you're actually in a generally good relationship with someone and still feel insecure, then it's time to . . .

1. Stop trying to read minds.

Most relationship problems and associated social anxieties start with bad communication, which in turn leads to attempted mind reading. Mind reading occurs when two people assume that they know what the other is thinking but they don't. This process of wondering and trying to guess what someone is thinking is a rapid route to feelings of insecurity and stress.

If someone says one thing, don't assume they mean something else. If they say nothing at all, don't assume their silence has some hidden, negative connotation. Likewise, don't make the people in your life try to read your mind. Say what you mean and mean what you say. Give the people in your life the information they need, rather than expecting them to know the unknowable.

It's also important to remember that you aren't supposed to know every little thing going on in the minds of others, even the people closest to you. When you stop trying to read their minds, you begin to respect their right to privacy. Everyone deserves the right to think private thoughts. Constantly asking, "What are you thinking?" can provoke a person to withdraw from a relationship to find space.

2. Stop looking for perfect relationships.

You will end up spending your entire life hopelessly seeking the right lover and the right friends if you expect them to be perfect. Even worse, the process of doing so will drive you mad, as you feel more and more insecure with every failed relationship that doesn't live up to your fantasy of perfection.

We're all seeking those special relationships that feel perfect for us, but if you've been through enough relationships, you begin to realize that there are no "perfect people" for you, just different flavors of imperfect ones. That's because we are all imperfect in some way. You yourself are imperfect in many ways, and you seek out relationships with people who are imperfect in complementary ways.

It takes a lot of life experience to grow fully into yourself and realize your own imperfections. And it isn't until you finally understand your deepest imperfections, your unsolvable flaws—the ones that truly define you—that you are able to proficiently select harmonious relationships. Only then do you finally know what you're looking for. You're looking for imperfect people who balance you out—the perfectly imperfect people for you.

3. Stop judging current relationships based on past ones.

Think about those times when you passed an unfair judgment on someone merely because they reminded you of someone from your past who treated you poorly. Sadly, some people pass judgments like these throughout the entire duration of their long-term relationships. Simply because they were once in a relationship with someone who was abusive or dishonest, or who left them, they respond defensively to everyone else who gets close to them, even though these new relationships have been nothing but kind and supportive.

If you carry old blueprints from the failed relationships of your past to your present relationships, you will build the same flawed structures that fell apart before. So if you suspect that you have been making unfair comparisons between your present relationships and a negative one from the past, take a moment to consciously reflect on the hurtful qualities of that old, negative relationship, and then think of all the ways your present relationships differ. This small exercise will help you let go of the old bricks and remind you that past pains are not indicative of present possibilities.

4. Stop inventing problems that don't exist.

Too often we amuse ourselves with anxious predictions, deceive ourselves with negative thinking, and ultimately live in a state of hallucination about worst-case scenarios. We overlook everything but the plain, downright simple, honest truth.

When you invent problems in your relationships, your relationships ultimately suffer. Insecurity is often the culprit. If you doubt yourself and you don't realize your own worth, you will assume others don't value you either, and you will interpret their gestures in a negative way.

For example, the insecure passenger does not trust anyone else to drive. They feel out of control. They imagine that the driver is not paying attention. Or they may even fantasize that the slight jolting of the driver stepping on the breaks is a sign of doom via an impending collision. They freak themselves out by assuming that the visions they have invented in their mind represent reality.

Try to keep in mind that there are normal idiosyncrasies to any relationship. There are ups and downs and mood changes, moments of affection and closeness and moments of friction. These ups and downs are normal. Wanting to be absolutely close and in sync all the time is like wanting to be a passenger in a parked car.

The next time you feel insecure, and you catch yourself stressing about problems that don't exist, stop yourself and take a deep breath. Then tell yourself, "This problem I'm concerned with exists only in my mind." Being able to distinguish between what you imagine and what is actually happening in your life is an important step toward self-confidence.

5. Stop focusing on the negatives.

There's no such thing as a perfect relationship. Even if it seems perfect now, it won't always be. Imperfection, however, is real and beautiful. The quality of the happiness between two people grows in direct proportion to their acceptance, and in inverse proportion to their intolerance and expectations. It's how two people accept and deal with the imperfections of their relationship that make it ideal.

Of course, this doesn't mean that you have to accept everyone into your life who is willing to accept you even if they are not right for you. But it does mean that if there are occasional difficulties in your relationships, you don't have to jump to the bold conclusion that the entire relationship is bad, and become so distressed that the relationship ends or so insecure that the other person questions your intentions.

No meaningful relationship will always work flawlessly all the time. Being too black-and-white about the quality and health of a relationship spells trouble. There will always be difficulties, but you can still focus on the good. Insecure people constantly look for signs of what's not working in their relationships. What you need to do is look for signs of what is.

Having an appreciation for how remarkable the people in your life are leads to good places—productive, fulfilling, peaceful places. So notice their strong qualities, cheer for their victories, and encourage their goals and ambitions. Challenge them to be the best they can be. Every day, acknowledge just how amazing they are.

10 Things You Need to Say Before It's Too Late

ABOUT A DECADE ago, a coworker of Marc's died in a car accident on the way home from work. During his funeral, several people from the office were in tears, saying kind things like, "I loved him. We all loved him so much. He was such a wonderful person." Of course, Marc started crying too. But he couldn't help wondering whether these people had told him that they loved him while he was alive, or whether it was only with death that this powerful word, "love," had been used without question or hesitation.

Marc vowed that day that he would never again hesitate to speak up to the people he cares about and remind them of how much he appreciates them. They deserve to know they give meaning to his life. They deserve to know he thinks the world of them.

But this wake-up call taught us something even bigger than that. It not only taught us to speak up to others; it taught us to speak up to ourselves too, about our attitudes, our self-respect, our dreams, and so on. Because the harsh truth is, we never know when everything will change. Or when great opportunities will pass. Or when everything we take for granted will be taken away. We don't know when later will be too late.

Don't let this reality depress you—let it motivate you. Let it push you to say what you've been meaning to say all along, to others and to yourself.

1. **"I love you."** Love rarely knows its own depth until it's taken away. So don't wait around. If you appreciate someone today, tell them. If you love someone today, show them. Hearts are often confused and broken by thoughtful words left unspoken and loving deeds left undone. There might not be a tomorrow. Today is the day to express your love and admiration.

2. **"Thank you."** For Marc's seventeenth birthday, many moons ago, his grandfather gave him four used flannel shirts he no longer needed. The shirts were barely worn and in flawless condition, and he told Marc that he thought they would look great on him. Sadly, Marc thought they were an odd gift at the time and wasn't thankful. He looked at his grandfather skeptically, gave him a crooked half smile, and moved on to the other birthday gifts. Marc's grandfather died two days later from a sudden heart attack. The flannel shirts were the last gifts Marc ever received from him, and Marc regrets the small thing he didn't say when he had the chance: "Thank you, Grandpa. That's so thoughtful of you."

3. **"I am a good person who is worthy of my own love and respect."** Human beings can withstand a week without water, two weeks without food, many years of homelessness . . . but not loneliness. It is the worst of all agonies. And what's the worst kind of loneliness? The kind you can't escape—when you are uncomfortable with yourself. The truth is, while a partner, or even just a friend, can add lots of beauty to your life, they can't fill a void that exists within you. You are solely responsible for your own fulfillment. If you feel hopelessly lonely whenever you're alone, it means you need to work on your relationship with yourself first.

4. "I can't always win, but I can always learn and grow." Don't confuse poor decision-making with your destiny. Own your mistakes. It's okay; we all make them. Learn from life experiences so they can empower you! What we call our destiny is really just our character, and that character can be enriched. Yes, the past has shaped your feelings and perspectives, but all this can be altered if you have the courage to reexamine how it has affected you.

5. "It's time to do something positive." The next time you have the urge to complain, stop and ask yourself what it is you truly want. Somewhere within each complaint is a genuine desire to improve things, but the complaint by itself is never enough to make it happen. So make the choice not to aggravate a bad situation with your complaints. Choose instead to improve it with your positive thoughts, ideas, and actions.

6. "I *can* do this!" The obstacle is never enough to stop you. What stops you is your belief that you can't get past the obstacle. The problem is not that you have too much of this or too little of that. The problem is, you're waiting for perfect conditions that don't exist. The achievements that really occur in life take place in reality. The things that really get done get done in an imperfect world. Don't make excuses for why you can't get it done. Focus on all the reasons why you must make it happen. There will always be challenges. And there will always be things you can do to grow beyond them.

7. "Their drama is *not* mine to deal with." Honestly, you can't save most people from themselves, so don't get sucked too deep into their drama. Those who make perpetual chaos of their lives won't appreciate you interfering with the commotion they've created, anyway. They want your sympathy, but they don't want to change. They don't want their lives fixed by *you*. They don't want their problems solved, their emotional addictions and distractions taken away, their stories resolved, or their messes cleaned up. Because what would they have left? They don't know, and they aren't ready to know yet. And it's not your job to tell them.

8. "I'm sorry." In this life, when you deny someone an apology, it may come back to haunt you when you find yourself begging for forgiveness. And it often happens just like that. Why? Because guilt festers. Don't do this to yourself. An apology is the best way to have the last word. The first to apologize is the strongest, and the first to move forward is the happiest. Always. And, of course, don't bother apologizing if you're just going to continue doing the things you said "sorry" for. Say it and mean it. Look the person in the eye when you say it, and feel it in your bones.

9. "I forgive you." A broken relationship that is mended through forgiveness can be even stronger than it was before. Of course, this isn't always the case. So remember that forgiveness doesn't necessarily lead to healed relationships. That's not the point. Some relationships aren't meant to be. Forgive anyway, for your own sake, and then let what's meant to be, *be*. Forgiveness allows you to focus on the future without combating the past. Without forgiveness, wounds can never be healed, and progress can never be made. What happened in the past is just one chapter. Don't close the book; just turn the page.

10. "Life right now is pretty darn good." Some people wait all day for 5:00 p.m., all week for Friday, all year for the holidays, all their lives for happiness. Don't be one of them. Don't wait until your life is almost over to realize how good it has been. The good life begins right now, when you stop waiting for a better one.

One Hard Thing You Must Admit Before Your Life Slips Away

WE'D LIKE TO share a story that Marc wrote about the night we met . . .

SHE HAS LIGHT brown hair, a seductive smile, and the most engaging set of hazel-green eyes I've ever seen. It's the kind of engaging I can't ignore—the kind that makes me want to engage too. Because she's mysterious. And I'm curious. And I need to know more.

Yet, I do my best to avoid making eye contact. So I stare down at the pool table and pretend to study my opponent's next move. But only long enough for her to look the other way, so I can once again catch a glimpse of magnificence.

I do this not because she intimidates me, but because I think she may be the girl Chad met last night. A wild night that, he said, "involved two bottles of port wine, chocolate cake, and sweaty bedsheets."

Then, just as her eyes unexpectedly meet mine, my opponent groans, "It's been your turn for like five minutes. Ya planning on going sometime tonight?" And the girl walks gracefully away.

So I continue to wonder, "Is she the port wine and chocolate cake girl? Gosh, she doesn't look like that kind of girl." But I don't wonder too long, because Chad enters the room and says, "Marc, there's someone I want you to meet." So I follow him into the kitchen and we bump right into her. "Oh, Angel," Chad says. "This is my buddy Marc."

And I smile from ear to ear and give off a little chuckle . . .

Because she's not the port wine and chocolate cake girl. But also because I had spent the past twenty minutes thinking about the port wine, and the chocolate cake, and the sweaty bedsheets.

Hours later, the party begins winding down. But the band is still playing, the two painters who have been painting a wall mural all evening are still painting, and Angel and I are still dancing.

"Are you tired?" I ask.

"No," Angel says. "Dancing is my outlet. When I dance, I transcend myself and the doubts that sometimes prevent me from being me. This evening has been enchanting, just dancing with you and being me."

So I twirl her around. And the drummer keeps drumming. The guitarist keeps strumming. The singer keeps singing. The painters keep painting. And now we're the only ones dancing.

As we continue to dance, she says, "I feel as if we're naked. And not just you and me, but the drummer, the guitarist, the singer, and the painters too. Everyone left in this room is naked . . . naked and free."

I smile and tell her that I agree. "We are naked. We are free."

As I know, we don't have to take our clothes off to be naked. Because moments of passionate presence flow into each other like port wine flows into chocolate cake. And if we let them, these moments can expose us completely, and continuously. And create climaxes that don't even require sex.

Because a true climax has little to do with sweaty bedsheets, and everything to do with the passion, love, and devotion we choose to invest in someone or something. In the same way, nakedness has little to do with how much clothing we wear, and everything to do with our

awareness in a given moment of time—an unfettered, present awareness that frees the mind and allows us to truly live the moment for all
it's worth.

After a few more songs, Angel asks if I'd like to join her out on
the front porch, where it's quieter. "Just so we can talk about life,"
she says.

I give her a little wink. "I love life in this crazy world! It is crazy,
isn't it?"

She smiles. "Yeah, a world in which we can be naked with our clothes
on and experience continuous climax without intercourse."

"Because instead we can achieve both with music, or paint, or dance,
or any form of avid self-expression," I add.

"You got it. Even the sincerity in this conversation is beginning
to work for me," she says, as we step out the front door and into the
moonlight.

The Presence It Takes to Change Your Life

Why did we just tell you that story?

Because sometimes we need a reminder.

As mentioned in the Introduction, we need to be reminded of the
beauty and sweetness of passionately absorbing oneself into the present moment—into the people, the dialogue, and the priceless little
events that exist there.

We need to be reminded of what it's like to be "naked" and "free."

Because too often, amid the hustle, we forget.

We forget to pay attention.

We forget to be grateful for the opportunity directly in front of us.

So Marc wrote a story about a night from our distant past that we
can remember and recite in vivid detail simply because we were completely present at the time.

We weren't distracted. We weren't in a rush to get somewhere better. We weren't resisting things, or trying to change them in any way.

We were 100 percent there.

And as a result, we allowed that night to change our lives.

Now, think about how this relates to your life . . .

Admitting the Hard Truth, and Embracing It

Where you are and what you're doing at any given moment is absolutely essential.

Because it is the only moment guaranteed to you.

You are not on your way somewhere else.

You are not progressing to a more important time or place.

The present is not just a stepping-stone: It is the ultimate destination, and you have already arrived.

This moment is where your greatest power lies.

This moment is your life!

It might seem obvious, but, again, we forget. And we know you do too.

All day, every day, many of us feel like the present isn't enough—like our life isn't worthy of our full presence. It's a hard truth, but we have to admit . . .

- We are continuously thinking about what's to come, as if it's not enough to appreciate what we have in front of us right now.
- We sit down to relax for a moment and then immediately feel the urge to read something on our phones, check social media, or text someone, as if relaxing for a moment isn't enough.
- We procrastinate when it's time to work, choosing more distractions, as if the process of doing good work isn't enough for us.

- We get annoyed with people when they fail to live up to our expectations, as if the reality of who they are isn't enough for us.
- We reject situations, people, and even ourselves, because we feel like we need more, more, more . . .

What If We Did the Opposite?

What if we accepted this moment, and everything and everyone in it (including ourselves), as exactly enough?

What if we admitted that life is slipping away right now, and saw the fleeting time we have as enough, without needing to share it on social media or capture it or alter it in any way?

What if we accepted the bad with the good, the letdowns with the lessons, the annoying with the beautiful, and the anxiety with the opportunity, as part of a package deal that this moment alone is offering us?

What if we paused right now and saw everything with perfect clarity and no distractions?

Keep thinking about it . . .

Would we live more meaningful and memorable lives?

Would we have more beautiful stories to cherish and share?

I think we would.

And thus, we think now is the best time to pay attention.

Now is the best time to look around and be grateful—for our health, our homes, our families, our friends, and our momentary opportunities.

Nothing lasts.

Everything is happening and changing before our eyes.

Let's do our best to be naked and free and aware of every little climactic moment, together.

SELF-LOVE & SELF-WORTH
QUESTIONS TO MAKE *YOU* THINK

When do you feel most alone, and what is your usual response to the feeling?

How has the fear of what other people might think of you interfered with your life?

In what ways have you struggled with rejection?

What kind of person do you love to be around?

What specific qualities do you look for in a friend or lover?

What relationship issues do you struggle with?

When it comes to your relationships, what makes you feel insecure?

Sit quietly with yourself, and ask: What will I regret never saying, both to the people I love and to myself?

Is it possible that all the bad or foolish things you've done have been forgiven and forgotten by everyone who matters in your life, except you?

What if you accepted this moment, and everything and everyone in it, as exactly enough?

PART TWO

Couples & Marriage

Communication Is Key

ONE OF THE best things you can do for your relationship with your life partner, whether you are married or not, is to create rituals that allow you to spend quality time together and check in with each other on a daily basis.

This is something we do in our marriage more than once a day. In the morning when we wake up, we ask each other, "What's on your mind today?" A lot of those mornings our son, Mac, is there and we include him in the conversation. At the end of the day we ask each other, "What was your favorite part of the day?" And during the day, at least four or five days a week, we go to the gym or take a jog together, and that time is not always spent talking about the big things, but it creates moments when we can have a small conversation, an opportunity to tune in with each other.

Communicating the things that make us happy is just as essential as communicating things that make us upset. We let each other know things like, "I loved it when we did this together. This made me feel good," or, "I really liked that you did this for me. It's so simple, but it made my day, so thank you" (like when Marc does the dishes at night before we go to bed!). Giving a compliment and communicating the positive aspects of our relationship is a way to let each other know when we appreciate something, and it inspires us to do that positive thing again.

We know that maintaining healthy communication in a relationship isn't easy, so start small: What's one small thing you can consistently do together, just you and your partner? You should be able to find ten minutes in your whole day for the person you love, and if you can have ten quiet minutes with them, then the space is there for everything that needs to happen, for the right conversations to take place, for the compliments to occur, for the questions to come up.

Say to your partner: Let's start with something as simple as a walk around the block or reading one or two pages of a book together every day and then discussing them. Angel reads short excerpts from books to us all the time, and a conversation always comes up as a result. We're talking about just a couple of pages. It takes ten minutes to read the pages and ask a question, and yet it's a wonderful ritual in our lives that brings us closer together.

How to Find the Perfect Man (or Woman)

THIS MORNING, OVER coffee, a good friend spilled her guts about all her failed attempts to find the perfect man. Although her story is about her unique, personal experiences, we couldn't help feeling like we'd heard the same story told by others in completely different circumstances a hundred times before. It's a heartbreaking tale about the endless quest for perfection that so many of us are on.

The Perfect Woman

Once upon a time, an intelligent, attractive, self-sufficient woman in her mid-thirties decided she wanted to settle down and find a husband. So she journeyed out into the world to search for the perfect man.

She met him in New York City at a bar in a fancy hotel lobby. He was handsome and well-spoken. In fact, she had a hard time keeping her eyes off him. He intrigued her. It was the curve of his cheekbones, the confidence in his voice, and the comfort of his warm, steady hands. But after only a short time, she broke things off. "We just didn't share the same religious views," she said. So she continued on her journey.

She met him again in Austin a few months later. This time, he was an entrepreneur who owned a small, successful record label that assisted local musicians with booking gigs and promoting their music. And she learned, during an unforgettable night, that not only did they share the same religious views, but also he could also make her laugh for hours on end. "But I just wasn't that physically attracted to him," she said. So she continued on her journey.

She met him again in Miami at a beachside café. He was a sports medicine doctor for the Miami Dolphins, but he easily could have been an underwear model for Calvin Klein. For a little while, she was certain he was the one! And all her friends loved him too. "He's the perfect catch," they told her. "But we didn't hang in the same social circles, and his high-profile job consumed way too much of his time and attention," she said. So she cut things off and continued on her journey.

Finally, at a corporate business conference in San Diego, she met the perfect man. He possessed every quality she had been searching for. Intelligent, handsome, spiritual, similar social circles, and a strong emotional and physical connection—absolutely perfect! She was ready to spend the rest of her life with him. "But unfortunately, he was looking for the 'perfect woman,'" she said.

Everything We've Ever Hoped For

As human beings, we often chase hypothetical, static states of perfection. We do so when we are searching for the perfect house, job, friend, or lover. The problem, of course, is that perfection doesn't exist in a static state. Because life is a continual journey, constantly evolving and changing. What is here today is not exactly the same tomorrow.

That perfect house, job, friend, or lover will eventually fade to a state of imperfection. Thus, the closest we can get to perfection is the experience itself—the snapshot of a single moment or vision held forever in our minds—never evolving, never growing. And that's not really what we want. We want something real! And when it's real, it won't ever be perfect. But if we're willing to work at it and open up, it could be everything we've ever hoped for, and more.

That Imperfect Man (or Woman)

The truth is, when it comes to finding the "perfect man" or "perfect woman" or "perfect relationship," the journey starts with letting go of the fantasy of "perfect." In the real world, you don't love and appreciate someone because they're perfect; you love and appreciate them in spite of the fact that they are not. Likewise, your goal shouldn't be to create a perfect life, but to live an imperfect life in radical amazement.

And when an intimate relationship gets difficult, it's not an immediate sign that you're doing it wrong. Intimate relationships are intricate, and are often toughest when you're doing them right—when you're dedicating time, having the hard conversations, compromising, and making daily sacrifices. Resisting the tough moments—the real moments—and seeing them as immediate evidence that something is wrong, or that you're with the wrong person, only exacerbates the difficulties. By contrast, viewing difficulties in a relationship as normal and necessary will give you and your partner the best chance to thrive together in the long run.

Again, there is no "perfect." To say that one waits a lifetime for their perfect soul mate to come around is an absolute paradox. People eventually get tired of waiting, so they take a chance on someone, and by the powers of love, compromise, and commitment they become soul mates, which takes nearly a lifetime to perfect.

This concept truly relates to almost everything in life too. With a little patience and an open mind, over time, we bet that imperfect house evolves into a comfortable home. That imperfect job evolves into a rewarding career. That imperfect friend evolves into a steady shoulder to lean on. And . . . that imperfect man or woman evolves into a "perfect" lifelong companion.

5 Questions That Will Save Your Relationships

When you don't ask sincere questions and talk it out, a lot of important stuff ends up never getting said.

"HEY, WHAT'S GOING on?" Marc asked.

"Not much," Angel said. "And how was your day?"

"It was okay," Marc said.

And just like that, our conversation would be over. For the longest time, this is exactly how we initiated conversations with each other at the end of long workdays.

Sure, we greeted each other and asked a few questions, but they weren't the right questions. They were habitual inquires that were stale and thoughtless. And not surprisingly, our conversations went nowhere. Which, in time, ended up hurting our relationship.

Thankfully, before it was too late, we learned to communicate more effectively. We learned that if we really wanted to deepen our relationship—if we really cared to know what's going on in each other's heads and hearts—we needed to ask better questions, and then really listen to each other's answers.

Specifically, we learned that we needed to ask questions that carry this fundamental message: "I'm not just checking the box here. I'm asking you because I really care how you feel and what you have to say. I really want to know *you*."

We want to help you ask questions that will save your relationships from a lot of grief. The bottom line is, if you don't want to have shallow, meaningless conversations with the important people in your life, you can't ask shallow, meaningless questions. A thoughtful, caring question is a key that will unlock the closed doors inside the people you love.

And although we learned this the hard way, we're happy we learned. We don't ask rote questions anymore, like "What's going on?" After several years of practicing more mindful question-asking, we now find ourselves naturally asking questions that strengthen our relationship. Let's take a look at some examples.

1. What made you feel good about yourself today?

Ask a loved one this question to help them celebrate what's right about their life right now.

It goes without saying, not every day will be good, but there will always be something good about every day. The key is to notice these things and celebrate them. Positivity is a choice. And the first step is celebrating what *can* be celebrated—the lessons, the laughs, and the love we've experienced along the way.

And best of all, when you help a loved one celebrate these things, your gesture alone becomes something worth celebrating and smiling about.

2. What have I done recently that helped you feel loved and appreciated?

If you struggle with this question in any way, here's a wake-up call for you: No matter how sure you are of someone's love, it is always nice to be reminded of it. Loving someone and having them love you back is the most precious phenomenon in the world, and it should be expressed as such. When you truly love someone, be loving in words and deeds every single day. Don't beat around the bush. Be straightforward.

If you appreciate someone today, tell them. If you adore someone today, show them. Hearts are often confused and broken by thoughtful words left unsaid and loving deeds left undone. There might not be a tomorrow. Today is the day to express your love and admiration.

3. What scares you about our relationship?

Truth be told, what often scares us the most is our vulnerability—how we are unavoidably vulnerable to each other when we choose to be in a relationship. So discuss this fact openly. Clear the air with the people you care about.

Consider the fact that all of us are subconsciously hardwired to connect with each other—through friendship, love, intimacy, and so forth—and your willingness to be vulnerable is the gateway to the affection you crave. But it takes serious courage to push the limits of your vulnerability, to dig deeper and deeper into the core of who you are as an individual, and not only love and accept the imperfect parts of yourself, but also expose them to someone else, trusting that this person will hold them lovingly.

Ultimately, to love is to be vulnerable, and to be willing to be vulnerable is to show your absolute greatest strength and your truest self. Finding and nurturing the right relationships that make this kind of love possible is a beautiful, lifelong process.

4. What has been making you feel alone and unworthy?

This is a difficult question to ask, and an even more difficult one to answer. But it's worth it.

Sometimes we feel as though the world is crashing down around us, as if the pain we are experiencing is unique to us in the moment. This, of course, is far from the truth. We are all in this together. The very demons that torment each of us, torment all of us. It is our challenges and troubles that connect us at the deepest level. Once we accept this, our relationships become a place where we can look each other in the eye and say, "I'm lost and struggling at the moment," and we can nod back at each other and say, "Me too," and that's okay. Because not being okay all the time is perfectly okay.

If you think about the people who have had the greatest positive effect on your life—the ones who truly made a difference—you will likely realize that they aren't the ones who tried to give you all the answers or solve all your problems. They're the ones who sat silently with you when you needed a moment to think, who lent you a shoulder when you needed to cry, and who tolerated not having all the answers but stood beside you anyway. Be this person for those you care about every chance you get.

5. What else hasn't been asked or discussed?

This is a simple question you have to ask yourself, as it leads to other relevant questions you might ask a person you're in a relationship with. It's about tapping into what you already know is going on in their life.

For example, if your husband had a big meeting today, you might ask, "How did you feel during the meeting today?" Or if your daughter has been talking about a new friend, ask her, "What did you say to your new friend during recess today?" Or if you know a friend's mom is fighting cancer, don't avoid the topic, address it directly: "How is your mom's chemo going?"

At the end of the day, you can't be afraid to dive deeper and have certain conversations. Remember that questions are like gifts—it's the thought behind them that the receiver feels. We have to know the receiver well enough to give the right gifts and ask the right questions. Generic gifts and questions are all right, but personal gifts and questions feel better. Because love is personal. The more attention and time you give to the questions you ask, the more beautiful the answers will become, and the stronger and stronger your relationships will grow.

4 Toxic Behaviors That Tear Couples Apart

OVER THE YEARS, through our coaching practice and premium course, we've worked with thousands of individuals and couples looking to fix their failing relationships, and we've learned a lot about what it takes to make this happen.

Whether you're working to fix your marriage, a dating relationship, or a friendship, you can do a lot of little things to keep your relationship on track. But many people are not aware of the most common toxic behaviors that tear relationships apart.

We can honestly say that when we listen to a couple talk for thirty minutes, we can determine, with close to 90 percent accuracy, whether their relationship will last in the long run (without major changes being made). The reason we can do this is simple: Most failing or failed relationships suffer from the same four basic behavioral issues:

1. Condemnation of a person's character

Complaints are fine. Disagreements are fine too. These are natural, focused reactions to a person's decisions or behavior. But when complaints and disagreements snowball into global attacks on the person, and not on their decisions or behavior, this spells trouble. For example: "They didn't call me when they said they would, not because they forgot, but because they're a horrible, wretched human being."

2. Hateful gestures

Frequent name-calling, threats, eye-rolling, belittling, mockery, hostile teasing, etc.—in whatever form, gestures like these are poisonous to a relationship because they convey hate. And it's virtually impossible to resolve a relationship problem when the other person is constantly getting the message that you hate them.

3. Denying responsibility

When you deny responsibility in every relationship dispute, all you're really doing is blaming your partner. You're saying, in effect, "The problem is never me. It's always you." This denial of responsibility just escalates the argument because there's a complete breakdown of communication.

4. The silent treatment

Tuning out, ignoring, disengaging, refusing to acknowledge, etc.—any variation of the silent treatment doesn't just remove the other person from the argument you're having with them; it ends up removing them, emotionally, from the relationship you have with them.

So What Makes a Relationship Flourish in the Long Run?

We want to give you a slightly different perspective with three key fundamentals:

- **Truly knowing each other**

Healthy couples are intimately familiar with each other's evolving stories. These couples make plenty of emotional room for their relationship, which means they sincerely listen to each other, they remember the major events they each have been through, and they keep up-to-date as the facts and feelings of their partner's reality changes. The key thing to remember is that nothing you can give is more appreciated than your sincere, focused attention—your full presence. Being with your partner, listening without a clock and without anticipation of the next event, is the ultimate compliment. It is indeed the most valued gesture you can make to them, and it arms you with the information you need to truly know them and support them in the long run.

- **Working out relationship issues with each other, not others**

This may seem obvious, but these days it's worth mentioning: *Never* post negatively about a loved one on social media. Fourteen-year-old schoolkids post negatively about their boyfriends, girlfriends, and friends on social media. It's a catty way to get attention and vent, when the emotionally healthy response is to talk your grievances over with them directly when the time is right. Don't fall into the trap of getting others on your side, because healthy relationships only have one side.

- **Using positive language in arguments**

Relationships flourish when both people are able to share their innermost feelings and thoughts in a positive way. One effective method of doing this during an argument is to try your best to avoid using the word "you" and instead use the word "I." This makes it much easier to express feelings and much harder to inadvertently attack the other person. Instead of saying, "You are wrong," try saying, "I don't understand."

Instead of telling them, "You always . . . ," try saying, "I often feel . . ." It's a subtle shift that can make a big difference.

Afterthoughts

The best relationships are not just about the good times you share. They're also about the obstacles you go through together, and the fact that you still say "I love you" in the end. And loving someone isn't just about saying it every day—it's showing it every day through your actions and behaviors.

6 Things Every Couple Should Stop Doing

WE OFTEN HEAR people complain about their husband, wife, or significant other, and their family life. We have also witnessed many failed marriages over the years, and they usually have something in common. If your relationship with your partner doesn't feel as healthy and happy as it once did, there's a good chance you both need to *stop* . . .

1. Being too busy to be present with each other.

The best gift you can give someone you love is the purity of your full presence. Presence is complete awareness, or paying full attention to "the now." If you do not find at least some amount of presence in the moments you share with your partner, it is impossible to listen, speak, compromise, or otherwise connect with them on a meaningful level.

To cultivate your presence, sit quietly for as long as you desire and put your full attention on your breath—thinking only of what each inhale and exhale feels like. Don't judge or resist your inner workings. Simply accept and breathe. Practice this a few times a day, and it will start to feel more natural. This way, when you are in the thick of a deep conversation with your partner, you can access that presence and listen without judgment or impatience, speak with clarity, and learn to fully connect and compromise.

Bottom line: Be present. Give your partner your full attention. Let them see their own beauty in your eyes. Let them find their own voice through your listening ears. Help them discover their own greatness in your presence.

2. Feeling too comfortable to compliment each other.

The secret to a healthy, lasting relationship is not about how many days, months, or years you've been together. It's about how much you truly love each other every day. You must directly express this love through your words and actions. It seems like such a small thing, but in our busy lives we often forget that a kind word, a helping hand, or just a smile and a quick "thank you" can create a bright spot in your partner's life.

A relationship lasts a lifetime only when two people make a choice to keep it and work for it. Tell your partner you love them every night, and prove it every day. These acts of love don't need to be extravagant; they just need to be true.

Also, acknowledging and appreciating each other's daily victories is one of the most loving things two people can do for each other. So before going to bed every night, take a moment to openly discuss and appreciate three things you each accomplished during the day, no matter how small. Compliment each other and celebrate together. What we focus on expands. What we appreciate, appreciates in value.

3. Resisting compromise.

Good relationships don't just happen, and they aren't built solely on a foundation of convenience. They take time, patience, effort, and two people who want to be together and are willing to meet in the middle.

When there's a disagreement, they find a solution that works for both parties—a compromise rather than a need for the other person to change or completely give in.

Ultimately, love is when another person's happiness is equally as important as your own. It's not only about romance, candlelit dinners, and walking hand in hand; it's about a lifetime of commitment and co-operation. Two people don't stay in love because they sleep in the same bed, but because they share the same foundation of honesty, trust, and respect.

4. Wanting to be right.

When it comes to closest relationships, you don't always have to be right. You just have to not be too worried about being wrong. Ask yourself, "Does it really matter?" Oftentimes it's far better to be kind than to be right.

Express your opinions freely and politely with your partner, remembering that if your purpose is to ridicule them or prove them wrong, it will only bring bitterness into your relationship. Respecting their opinion, without judging or jumping to conclusions, always carries more weight than simply being right.

Bottom line: Life is so much better when you focus on being happy together, rather than worrying about who is more right as an individual.

5. Hiding personal flaws and problems from each other.

You attract a person by the qualities you show them, you keep them around based on the qualities you truly possess. Problems and flaws are a part of everyone's life. If you try to hide them, you don't give the person who loves you a chance to truly know you and love you fully.

As flawed as you might be, as out of place as you sometimes feel, and as lacking as you believe you are, you don't have to hide the imperfect pieces of yourself from your partner. They see your flaws as features that make you interesting, and they see your problems simply as a sign that you're human too.

By hiding things from your partner, you allow small problems to escalate and dominate both your life and your relationship. If you make a mistake, it might be irritating, but don't bury it inside you. Be open about it, address it, and move on. Our problems are really our blessings if we use them to grow stronger, both as individuals and as couples.

6. Trying to get even as a replacement for forgiveness.

Getting even doesn't help a relationship heal. If you're feeling pain, don't take action that creates even more pain. Don't try to cover darkness with darkness. Find the light. Act out of love. Do something that will enable you to move forward toward a more fulfilling reality.

If your partner makes a mistake that hurts you, and you want your relationship to grow beyond it, you have to start with forgiveness. Without it, the potential for long-term happiness in a relationship is impossible.

You don't forgive your partner because you're weak; you forgive them because you're strong enough to know that human beings make mistakes. Forgiveness is giving up your craving to hurt them for hurting you. It doesn't mean you're erasing the past or forgetting what happened. It means you're letting go of the resentment and pain, and instead choosing to learn from the incident and move forward with your life . . . and hopefully move forward with your relationship too.

Afterthoughts

The greatest relationships take a great deal of work. They don't just happen or maintain themselves. They thrive only when two people make an effort and take the risk of sharing what's going on in their heads and hearts.

Keep in mind that every couple has ups and downs, every couple argues, and that's the way it should be—you're in a partnership, and partnerships can't function without regular communication and compromise. When you don't talk it out, a lot of important stuff ends up not getting said.

Above all, remember that it's not all about you. There is greatness in doing something you wouldn't otherwise do, all for the sake of someone you love.

10 Things Happy Couples Do Differently

IT'S IMPORTANT TO understand that love is not just about finding the right person—it's about working with them to create the right relationship. We have met and worked with couples at both ends of the spectrum over the years, and we've found that the happiest couples, or the unhappy couples who successfully turn things around, are able to create loving, lasting relationships by doing the following:

1. They make plenty of time for each other.

Nothing is more vital to the bond you share with someone than simply being there for them. Too often we underestimate the power of a thoughtful question and a listening ear that's fully present and focused. Although it's a simple act, it may very well be the most powerful act of caring—one that has the potential to turn a relationship around.

When we pay attention to each other, we breathe new life into each other. With frequent attention and affection, our relationships flourish, and we as individuals grow stronger. This is the side effect of a good relationship—we help heal each other's wounds and support each other's strengths.

Bottom line: Stay in close touch with what's going on in your partner's life, communicating openly on a regular basis. Not because it's convenient, but because they are worth the extra effort.

2. They don't beat around the bush.

No matter how sure you are of someone's love, it's always nice to be reminded of it. When you truly love someone, be loving in words and deeds every single day. Don't tiptoe around. Be straightforward with the love you have to give.

3. They meet in the middle and work together.

The most important trip you will ever take in life is meeting your partner halfway. You will achieve far more by working with them, rather than working alone or against them. That's what healthy relationships are all about—teamwork. It really is a full circle. The strength of a relationship depends on the strength of its two members, and the strength of each member in the long run depends on the quality of the relationship.

Anyone who helps you to make your half-hearted attempts more wholehearted through passion, love, and teamwork is a precious friend and teacher, and thus makes a great partner. Take the lead and *be* this partner. Make an effort to work closely with your significant other and conquer the world together.

4. Their actions consistently back up their claims of love.

Actions often speak much louder than words. When you love someone, it's important to act accordingly. They will be able to tell how you feel about them simply by the way you treat them over the long term.

You can say "sorry" a thousand times, or say "I love you" as much as you want, but if you're not going to prove that the things you say are true, they aren't. If you can't show it, your words are not sincere.

And remember, how much you do for your loved ones isn't as important as the love you put into what you do for them. Learn what matters most to them and make a habit of it.

5. They respect each other's humanness.

All humans are imperfect. At times, the confident lose their confidence, the patient misplace their patience, the generous act selfishly, and the knowledgeable second-guess what they know.

We all have our moments. So stand beside the people you love through their trying times of imperfection, and offer yourself the same courtesy; if you aren't willing to, you don't deserve to be around for the perfect moments either.

6. They focus on what they like about each other.

What you focus on grows stronger. When you focus on a person's wonderful qualities, you have a wonderful relationship with them. When you focus on a person's not-so-wonderful qualities, you have a not-so-wonderful relationship with them. When you focus on the benefits of a situation, you get to enjoy them. When you focus on the drawbacks, you gain nothing but a frown.

The bottom line is that you see what you want to see, and what you see determines the health of your relationships. Your attitude is a little thing that makes a massive difference. Don't be the stubborn one who makes it a point to not see the good in your partner.

7. There is far more between them than physical attraction.

Becoming infatuated with someone simply for what they look like on the outside is like choosing your favorite food based on color instead of taste. It makes no sense. It's innate, invisible, unquantifiable characteristics that create lasting attraction. There must be common ground in your interests and outlooks on life.

Much like some people enjoy the smell of mint while others prefer the scent of cinnamon, there is an undeniable, magnetic draw that attracts you to the qualities of certain people, places, and things. Sometimes it's even the scars your soul shares with them that reels you in and creates the very hinges that hold you together in the long run.

8. They resolve conflicts through love, not retaliation.

If you're disappointed with yourself or frustrated with your partner, the answer is not to take it out on the world around you. Retribution, whether it's focused on yourself or others, brings zero value into your life. The way beyond the pain from the past is not with vengeance, mockery, bullying, or retaliation but with present love.

Forgive the past, forgive yourself, forgive your partner, and love the present moment for what it's worth. There are plenty of beautiful things to love right now; you just have to want to see them. Loving is never easy, especially when times are tough; yet it is easily the most powerful and positively enduring action possible.

9. They open up to each other, especially in trying times.

Let your partner in when you're in a dark place. Open up to them completely. Don't expect them to solve your problems; just allow them to face your problems with you. Give them permission to stand beside you. They won't necessarily be able to pull you out of the dark place you're in, but the light that spills in when they enter will at least show you which way the door is.

Above all, the important thing to remember is that you are not alone. No matter how bizarre or embarrassed or pathetic you feel about your own situation, your partner is in your life and has dealt with similar emotions and wants to help you. When you hear yourself say, "I am alone," it's just your insecurities trying to sell you a lie.

10. They are committed to growing together.

It's not about finding someone to lose yourself in—it's about meeting someone to find yourself in. When you connect with someone special, especially a lifelong partner, this person helps you find the best in yourself. In this way, neither of you actually meet the best in each other; you both grow into your best selves by spending time together and nurturing each other's growth.

When you honestly think about what you and your partner add to each other's lives, you will often find that instead of giving or taking things from each other (advice, answers, material gifts, etc.), you two have chosen to share in each other's joy and pain, and to experience life together through good times and bad. No matter what, you two are there for each other, growing and learning as one.

Afterthoughts

The best relationships are not just about the good times you share. They're also about the obstacles you go through together, and the fact that you still say "I love you" in the end. And loving someone isn't just about saying it every day. It's showing it every day in every way.

6 Ways Happy Couples Deal with Disagreements Differently

EVERY COUPLE DISAGREES from time to time. Perfect compatibility is not possible, but sensibly working though our differences is.

Talk to any set of grandparents (or great-grandparents) whose relationship has withstood the tests of time, and they will tell you that the best relationships are not just about the good times you share. They're also about the obstacles you go through together, the disagreements you compromise on, and the fact that you express your love openly.

Based on our fifteen-year relationship with each other, and our joint experience coaching thousands of individuals and couples over the past decade, here's what we've learned about how happy couples deal with disagreements:

1. They are committed to dealing with disagreements positively.

Often it is easiest to run from a disagreement, especially if you're not a confrontational person by nature. But remember, this isn't about you or whether or not you feel like dealing with your differences. It's about what your relationship needs in order to grow and thrive in the long run. So put these needs ahead of your own. Both partners must be committed to dealing with their disagreements, because running from them will only make matters more difficult to deal with down the road.

2. They attack their disagreements, not each other.

Disagreements are fine, and arguments are too. These are natural, focused reactions to a person's decisions or behavior. Problems arise when disagreements and arguments snowball into global attacks on the other person, and not on their decisions or behavior.

Even when it's hard to think clearly in the heat of the moment, you have to take a deep breath and remember that your partner is on your team. Always support each other, even when you don't see eye to eye. Don't take your stress out on each other. Keep your focus on the problematic disagreement and attack it together by talking it out and reaching a deeper understanding.

3. They practice intentional communication.

Your partner is not a mind reader. Share your thoughts openly. Give them the information they need rather than expecting them to know it all. The more that remains unspoken, the greater the risk for problems. Start communicating clearly. Don't try to read their mind, and don't make them try to read yours. Most problems, big and small, within a relationship start with broken communication.

Also, don't listen so that you can reply—listen to understand. Open your ears and mind to your partner's concerns and opinions without judgment. Look at things from your partner's perspective as well

as your own. Try to put yourself in their shoes. Even if you don't understand exactly where they're coming from, you can still respect them. So
turn your body toward them, look them in the eyes, turn off the com-
puter, and put away your phone. Doing so demonstrates that you actually want to communicate with your partner and hear what they have to
say; this reinforces the sort of supportive environment that's crucial for
conflict resolution.

4. They let each other save face.

Marc's grandmother once told him, "When somebody backs themselves
into a corner, look the other way until they get themselves out, and then
act as though it never happened." Allowing your partner to save face in
this way, and not reminding them of what they already know isn't their
most intelligent behavior, is an act of great kindness. This is possible
when you realize that your partner behaves in such ways because they
are in a place of momentary suffering. They react to their own thoughts
and feelings, and their behavior often has nothing directly to do
with you.

At some point we all inevitably have unreasonable mood swings.
We all have bad days. Giving your partner some room to save face, and
not taking things personally when they're occasionally upset, cranky,
or having a bad day, is a priceless gift.

Even if you are unquestionably right and your partner is unquestionably wrong, when emotions are flying high and you force them to
lose face, you're simply bruising their ego. You're accomplishing nothing but diminishing their own worth in their own eyes. Do your best to
let your partner preserve their dignity. Give them space, let the emotions settle, and then have a rational conversation using the positive
communication tactics discussed above in point number 2.

5. They are willing to make sacrifices for each other.

True love involves attention, awareness, discipline, effort, and being able to care about someone and sacrifice for them, continuously, in countless petty, little, unsexy ways every day. You put your arms around them and love them regardless, even when they're not seeing things your way. And, of course, they do the same for you.

6. They expect to disagree with each other on some things, and they're okay with it.

Again, differences of opinion (even major ones) don't destroy relationships—it's how a couple deals with their inevitable differences that counts.

Some couples waste years trying to change each other's mind, but this can't always be done, because many of their disagreements are rooted in fundamental differences of opinion, personality, or values. By fighting over these deep-seated differences, they succeed only in wasting their time and running their relationship into the ground.

So how do healthy, happy couples deal with disagreements that can't be resolved?

They accept one another as is. These couples understand that differences are an inevitable part of any long-term relationship, in the same way chronic physical difficulties are inevitable as we grow older and wiser. These problems are like a weak knee or a bad back—we may not want these problems, but we're able to cope with them, to avoid situations that irritate them, and to develop strategies that help us deal with them. Psychologist Dan Wile said it best in his book *After the Honeymoon*: "When choosing a long-term partner, you will inevitably be choosing a particular set of unsolvable problems that you'll be grappling with for the next ten, twenty, or fifty years."

Bottom line: The foundation of love is to let those we care about be unapologetically themselves, and to not distort them to fit our own egotistical ideas of who they should be. Otherwise we only fall in love with our own fantasies, and thus miss out entirely on their true beauty. So save your relationship from needless stress. Instead of trying to change your partner, give them your support and grow together, as individuals.

9 Old-Fashioned Relationship Habits We Should Bring Back

RECENTLY WE WERE sitting on a park bench eating a sandwich for lunch when an elderly couple pulled their car up under a nearby oak tree. They rolled down the windows and turned up some funky jazz music on the car stereo. Then the man got out of the car, walked around to the passenger side, opened the door for the woman, took her hand and helped her out of her seat, and guided her about ten feet away from the car, and they slow-danced to a song under the oak tree.

It was such a beautiful moment to witness.

Not long after that, a reader named Cory emailed with the question: "Any good, old-fashioned advice for a struggling relationship?"

So in honor of that beautiful elderly couple, and in service of Cory's relationship situation, here are nine old-fashioned habits we need to bring back into our relationships:

1. Spend quality time together with no major agenda and no technology.

Put down the smartphone, close the laptop, and enjoy each other's company, face-to-face, the old-fashioned way.

There are few joys in life that equal a good conversation, a genuine laugh, a long walk, a friendly dance, or a big hug shared by two people who care about each other. Sometimes the most ordinary things can be made extraordinary just by doing them with the right people. So choose to be around these people, and choose to make the most of your time together.

Don't wait to make big plans. Make your time together the plan. Communicate openly on a regular basis. Get together face-to-face, or perhaps on Zoom or FaceTime, as often as possible. Not because it's convenient to do so, but because you know your partner is worth the extra effort.

2. Be fully present when you're in the presence of others.

One of the best feelings in the world is knowing your presence and absence both mean something to someone. And the only way to let your loved ones know this is to show them when you're with them.

In your relationships and interactions with others, nothing you can give is more appreciated than your sincere, focused attention—your full presence. Being with someone, listening without watching the clock or anticipating the next event, is the ultimate compliment. It is indeed the most valued gesture you can make to another human being.

Your friends and family are too beautiful to ignore. So give them the gift of *you*—your time, undivided attention, and your kindness. That's better than any other gift—it won't break or get lost, and will always be remembered.

3. Express your sincere appreciation for loved ones every chance you get.

No matter how sure you are of someone's appreciation and admiration, it's always nice to be reminded of it. So if you appreciate someone today, tell them. Just because they are reliable and there when you need them doesn't mean you should fail to give thanks and appreciation on a regular basis. To value someone too lightly is to risk missing the depth of their goodness before they're gone.

Sadly, it is often only when we are tragically reminded of how short life is—that today could easily be our last with someone we love—that we start to appreciate every day we have together. Let this lesson sink in now. Don't wait until it's too late to tell the people you love how much you appreciate them.

4. Work together and help each other grow.

There is no soul mate or best friend out there who will solve all your problems. There is no love at first sight that lasts without work and commitment. But there are, however, people out there worth fighting for. Not because they're perfect, but because they're imperfect in all the ways that are right for you. You complement each other's flaws in a way that allows your souls to unite and work together more effectively as one.

You will know when you meet one of these people, when through them you meet the very best in yourself.

5. Focus on inner beauty.

When you get to really know someone, most of their prominent physical characteristics vanish in your mind. You begin to dwell in their energy, recognize their scent, and appreciate their wit. You see only the essence of the person, not the shell.

That's why you can't fall in love with physical beauty. You can lust after it, be infatuated by it, or want to embody it. You can love it with your eyes and your body for a little while, but not your heart in the long-term. Thus, when you really connect with a person's inner self, most physical imperfections become irrelevant.

6. Tell the truth.

Too many prefer gentle lies to hard truths. But make no mistake: In the end, it's better to be hurt by the truth than to be comforted by a lie. Relationships based on lies always die young.

Lying is a cumulative process too. So be careful. What starts as a small, seemingly innocent lie (possibly even told with the intention of not hurting anyone) quickly spirals into a mounting false reality where the biggest factor preventing you from sharing the truth is not getting the reputation as a liar. We lie to one another, but even more so we lie to ourselves, most often to protect our oh-so fragile egos. We may even be inclined to lie to ourselves while reading this, not wanting to admit how often we have eluded the truth.

7. Apologize when you know you should.

Take personal responsibility for your wrongdoings. Apologize, and make sure your apology is sincere. Say it and mean it. Don't bother apologizing if you're just going to continue doing the things you said "sorry" for doing. Never ruin an apology with an excuse. Excuses are *not* apologies.

8. Overdeliver on your promises.

Be committed. Commitment means staying devoted to and keeping your promises, long after the time and mood you made the promises in has left you. Doing so is vital to your relationships and long-term success in every imaginable walk of life.

So don't just say it, show it. Don't just promise it, prove it. Better yet, overdeliver on all your promises. Supply far more than what's required. Remember that no one has ever become poor by giving. Whenever you can, go out of your way to do something nice and unexpected for your significant other, especially if he or she is in no position to re-pay you anytime soon.

9. Be loyal.

Stand by those you care about in their darkest moments, not because you want to stand in the dark, but because you don't want them to ei-ther. Brave the shadows alongside them until they're able to find the light. On the flip side, stand by these same people on their sunniest days, not because you want to scorch your skin, but because you're not afraid to let them shine bright.

In other words, be loyal. Remaining faithful in your relationships is never an option but a given. Loyalty means the world to the people who love you. When someone believes in you enough to lift you up, try not to let them down. You can't promise to be there for someone for the rest of their life, but you can sincerely be there for them for the rest of yours.

How to Make Love Last: The Best Relationship Advice from 45 Years of Marriage

WHEN WE WERE first falling in love, Marc went to his parents' house one evening for some much needed relationship advice. The advice they gave Marc that evening was truly wise, but even more important was the family ritual born that day. Every year since—now nineteen years and counting—Marc has pestered his parents (they love it) on their wedding anniversary and asked them for a new relationship tip or two, and he records their advice in his journal.

Here we want to share a cleaned-up version of Marc's parents' relationship tips. These are the little things they do—the rituals—that have helped their relationship last for forty-five years and counting. Perhaps you will find as much value in their wisdom as Angel and I have.

1. Stand strong on your own first.

As we mentioned earlier in this book, if your happiness is dependent on the constant validation and approval of your partner, then you are giving away far too much of your power. It's human nature to want to be loved and admired, to want to be included, but it's damaging to your self-esteem and emotional strength if it's something you have to constantly beg for.

The key is to nurture your own inner strength, then bring it into your relationship.

Again, think of your relationship as a home you live in. Whether you like your home or not doesn't depend on how the furniture is arranged; it's how you arrange your mind. You have to decide to love yourself in it and then radiate this inner love outward.

Remember that all the love and validation you need is yours to give yourself. So the next time you feel pressured to be a people pleaser, try taking a deep breath and reminding yourself that you don't owe anyone your constant justification—not even your partner. Revel in the reality that you get to choose. You have the authority to decide how to spend your time and energy. And here's the real beauty of it: When you don't owe anyone anything—when you're self-reliant—you're free to give and receive love from the heart, without baggage.

Come from this place of wholeness, of inner strength and independence, and then love your partner. Not because you need them to love you back, not because you're desperate to be needed, but because loving them is a miraculous thing to do.

2. Maintain a solid foundation of mutual acceptance.

Above all, acceptance means two people agree to disagree with each other on some things, and they're perfectly okay with it. Differences of opinion, even major ones, don't destroy relationships—it's how people in a relationship deal with their inevitable differences that counts.

You won't always see things eye to eye, and that's okay. Sometimes you just need to choose to be wrong, not because you really are wrong, but because you value your relationship more than you value your pride.

3. Face disagreements openly and with positive language.

When disagreements in a relationship arise, the easiest thing to do is to run away, especially if you're not a confrontational person by nature. But you have to catch yourself, because this isn't just about you and whether or not you feel like dealing with your differences. It's about what your relationship needs in order to grow and thrive in the long run. You have to put your relationship's needs ahead of your own sometimes. Both people must be committed to dealing with disagreements openly, because running from them will only make matters more difficult to deal with down the road.

4. Seek, support, and accept personal growth in each other's lives.

You know how to tell if something is alive and well? You look for evidence of growth.

Healthy lifelong relationships contain two people who are committed to lifelong learning and growth. They're curious about things. They're keen to learn from the world and from each other. And because of their love for learning, they afford each other the freedom to develop as individuals within the relationship.

Marc's parents have seen many unhappy relationships that were caused primarily by one or both people being stubbornly clingy. In a nutshell, these stubbornly clingy people didn't want their friends or partners to change. But here's the simple truth: Change is a part of the universe, and human beings are no exception. If you want to have a successful relationship, you've got to embrace personal growth, and all the changes that come with it, with open arms.

5. Let love be a daily practice.

This final point encompasses the previous four, and then some. In a healthy long-term relationship, two people love each other more than they need each other. Because of this, the relationship itself becomes a safe haven to practice love. And love, ultimately, is a practice—a daily rehearsal of honesty, presence, communication, acceptance, forgiveness, and heartfelt patience.

Sadly, too often we forget the practicing part, and we default instead to treating love like it's a guaranteed destination we can jump to whenever we have time. We want to arrive at that "perfect" loving feeling in a relationship without putting in the work. And when it doesn't work out that way, we assume the relationship itself is broken. But this is missing the whole point of a relationship—and the whole point of love.

Again, love is a practice. It's showing up for all the unexpected and inconvenient moments of a relationship, taking a deep breath, and asking yourself, "What part of love needs to be practiced here?" The answer will vary from one encounter to the next, in a continuous stream of tenderness, affection, and wisdom you could never have dreamed of or perfectly planned for upfront.

Afterthoughts

We have been together for nearly two decades now—we've been through a lot together—and we love each other more and more with each passing day. And we are convinced the relationship advice above is the reason why. It's some of the best, most practical, and hard-won relationship advice there is.

Talk to any set of grandparents—like Marc's parents—whose relationship has withstood the tests of time, and they will tell you that the best relationships are not just about the good times you share. They're also about the obstacles you go through together, the disagreements you compromise on, and the fact that you still say "I love you" in the end. And loving someone isn't just about saying it every day; it's about showing it every day through actions and behaviors, even when you and your partner aren't seeing things eye to eye.

COUPLES & MARRIAGE QUESTIONS TO MAKE *YOU* THINK

What resonates with you most about finding the "perfect" man or woman?

Any thoughts on perfectionism's harmful role in relationships?

In your experience, what are some common misunderstandings, or thinking traps, that hurt intimate relationships?

What toxic relationship behaviors and circumstances do you try to avoid?

What positive habits do you foster together?

What harmful habits have you observed in couples, growing up or as an adult, that you don't want to emulate in your relationships?

In your experience, what helps create a happy relationship?

What's on your mind right now regarding your relationship?

Think about a longtime happy couple in your life—what do you notice they do that you think your relationship would benefit from?

What is the number one ingredient to building the right relationships?

PART THREE

Children &
Family

Kids Have Opinions Too

WE DO NOT believe that a child should be seen and not heard. We tell our son, Mac, that he's a valuable part of our family, and he has a voice as much as we do. There are three of us in our family, and each person gets a vote, and we all have an equal say in expressing our needs and wants.

We have talked about creating space for each other to share by asking the right questions, and we do this with Mac all the time as well. We ask him questions like

- What do you want to do today and why?
- What's on your mind today?
- What made you happy today?
- What made you feel uncomfortable today?
- Did anything make you laugh today?
- What made you sad today?

It's amazing what comes out of a five-year-old's mind sometimes, and you'd be surprised at how asking these questions, targeted at specific emotions, will bring up stories that he shares with us simply because, by asking, we invite him to be a part of our conversation.

Often these conversations happen during our planned family time, which is something we schedule on the calendar: time for us to be together as a family, enjoying each other and getting to know each other. Now, the time is scheduled, but that doesn't mean we have that time booked with dozens of activities.

We are careful to not overwhelm Mac, or ourselves, with extracurricular activities. We've learned that if parents are overwhelmed by all the activities, then the kids are too. Don't get us wrong—extracurricular activities are great. But just because you're watching them perform at a game or practice doesn't mean that it's quality time for you and your child. Instead, we figure out what makes sense for us and keep our time together flexible.

Here's an example. We had some friends who were driving back home on Interstate 95 from North Florida, near our house, and they called us at three o'clock on a Sunday afternoon to say they'd love to swing by for a couple of hours to say hello. They expected us to say no, thinking we would be busy. But we said, absolutely—come over. We had a joyous time. Their son is Mac's age, and we get to see them only once every couple of months, so it was a wonderful surprise. We had a great evening together, and we can say yes to experiences like this when they come up because we are not overbooked.

Building a family life and parenting is often about doing the hard thing, which is to create space for listening to each other, especially to your kids. Schedule the time without overscheduling activities. Ask the kids questions. Ask them what they want to do. Don't talk over them. Let them have an opinion even at four or five years of age. When they're thirteen or fourteen years old, let their opinion be considered fully, like you are listening to an adult's opinion.

One Priceless Lesson
We Often Forget About
Love and Life

Everything We Need

Jose's wife, Maria, was born in a one-bedroom, home on the out skirts of Playa del Carmen, Mexico. It was a fine little home, but her father, Oscar, wanted a "real" house. So he worked two jobs—a sixty-hour-a-week factory job, and then another twenty hours or so a week as a carpenter.

Oscar saved 50 percent of his income for over a decade to build his family a four-bedroom house—like the ones in the better parts of town. He put half of his family's savings in a local community bank, and he tucked the other half away in a safe he kept hidden on their property.

On the morning Oscar planned to break ground on his family's new house, the local community bank shuttered its doors, just hours after law enforcement declared that the bank was running an illegal (and uninsured) Ponzi scheme. Ninety percent of the deposits Oscar had made were lost. Then, the very next day, their little home was robbed at gunpoint. In exchange for his family's safety, Oscar offered the rest of the money he had hidden in the safe.

In the short window of thirty-six hours, the family lost the vast majority of their savings from years of hard work. That night, for the first time, Maria's mother, Olga, watched Oscar cry. She approached Oscar, with their infant daughter cradled and rocking in her arms, and said, "It's just money. And it's just a house. We have so much more than that. We have a truly loving home."

Oscar looked at Olga, dried his eyes, and nodded his head in agreement. He spent the rest of the night with his baby daughter, holding her tight to his chest, reminding himself that he might not be able to give his family the house he dreamed of, but he could continue to give them a truly loving home.

And for the nine years that followed, Maria grew up in that small, loving, one-bedroom home. After the first year, a sister, Andrea, joined her. After the third year, a brother, Roberto, joined too. The memories they share of that time are truly heartwarming.

For example, every day of Maria's early grade school years, she remembers her father coming home from work just before dinner, giving her and her siblings individual hugs and kisses, and then asking them two questions: "Are you loved? Do you have love in your heart?" All three children would nod their heads, smiling. Then he'd gather them all up in a big group hug and call out, "Me too! We are blessed! We have everything we need!"

With That House

Even though Oscar sincerely believed what he said to his children, he was still pursuing his dream of building a larger and more comfortable house for his family. And nine years after losing all their savings, Oscar had once again saved enough money to begin building that new house twenty feet behind their little one-bedroom home. He started with framing out the foundation of the kitchen that Maria's mother had always quietly dreamed of.

One concrete block at a time, paycheck by paycheck, Oscar slowly but steadily built the house he'd come so close to building nearly a decade before. First the kitchen, a large family room, and two bathrooms. Then a master bedroom, bedrooms for each of the children, and a nice covered front patio.

In 2002, when Jose met Maria, and started falling in love with her, Oscar was still building that house. Soon thereafter, he put the last few finishing touches on it. The entire family celebrated for weeks on end. And nowadays, Oscar and Olga still celebrate holidays and special occasions at the house, with all three of their children, and their children's families, several times a year.

But this story's priceless lesson has nothing to do with that house.

"Just a Bonus"

The first day Jose met Maria's family, he noticed how sincerely loving and happy the whole family was. He praised Oscar for the beautiful family he had and asked him what the secret was. Oscar spent hours sharing interesting, heartfelt stories about why his family was the luckiest one in the world. But he never shared all the details about how their house was built.

In fact, after years of knowing Maria and her family, traveling with them, and even living with them for a short time, Jose had never been told about how their family's house came to be. Jose asked questions about the building methods on a few occasions. And he received replies about the construction.

It wasn't until after Jose and Maria got married and closed on their own first house—in Miami, Florida—that Oscar took Jose for a long walk. He asked Jose about the details, and Jose excitedly shared information about their new neighborhood and the house. Oscar listened intently, smiled, and then, finally, he shared the story you've just read about.

"My daughter does not need a house," Oscar concluded. "She needs a truly loving home. And when you fill that home with children, your children will need exactly the same. If you provide that, no matter how big or small your actual house is, your children will always want to come home to you. The rest is just a bonus."

WE KNOW THIS story because Jose is one of Marc's best friends. We share it here as a reminder of what truly matters in the relationships we are building with our children and our family.

9 Things Happy Families Do Differently

RECENTLY, WE HAD one of Marc's old friends from high school over to our home for dinner. After a delicious meal, he and Marc chatted for a couple of hours in the family room and caught up on old times. And as they wrapped things up, he said to Marc, "I admire you. I admire the love in this home—the obvious love between you and Angel. I admire the close relationships you've built and nurtured. When I'm here, it feels like I'm part of the family. Nurturing a happy family is one of the things I never got around to. So it was great to see it, feel it, and be a part of it tonight. Thank you."

This got us thinking: What does nurturing a happy family really mean? What are some things happy families do differently? Here are some thoughts to consider:

1. Every day, every member chooses to be part of the family.

First and foremost, family isn't always blood. They're the people in your life who appreciate having you in theirs—the ones who encourage you to improve in healthy and exciting ways, and who not only embrace who you are now but also embrace and embody who you want to be. Family members can be your best friends. And best friends, whether or not they're related to you by blood, can be your family.

Family is built with love; it's not determined by legal documents. Families grow from the heart, through mutual love and respect. The only time family becomes nullified is when the ties in the heart are cut. If you cut the ties, these people are no longer your family. So build and maintain ties with the right people and nurture them with love every day.

2. Family members go out of their way for each other.

Family bonds are tied with true love, and true love involves attention, awareness, discipline, effort, and being able to care about someone and sacrifice for them, continuously, in countless little ways, every day. Be willing to schedule them in, even when it's inconvenient.

3. Family sticks together through thick and thin.

"Being family" is also about supporting each other through life's inevitable changes. It's knowing that your family will be there watching out for you through thick and thin. Nothing and no one else will give you that. Not your career. Not your boss. Not your clients. Not money. Not fame.

And remember, timing is everything. There is a time for silence, a time to let go and allow your loved ones to launch themselves into their own future, and a time to cheer for their victories or help them pick up the pieces when things don't go as planned.

4. Everyone is permitted to be true to themselves.

The deepest craving of human nature is the need to be appreciated as is. Sometimes we try to be sculptors, constantly carving out of others the image of what we want them to be—what we think we need, love, or desire. But these actions and perceptions are against reality, against their benefit and ours, and always end in disappointment—because it does not fit them.

5. Everyone takes responsibility for their own happiness.

Happiness is a choice that comes from within. Being happy doesn't mean everything is perfect; it means you've decided to look beyond the imperfections. There are choices you can make every day to feel the effects of happiness. Choose to do something meaningful. Choose to take care of your body. Choose to be around the right people. Choose to have a good attitude. Choose to express gratitude. Choose to forgive. Choose to focus on what you have, not on what you don't.

Begin today by taking responsibility for your own happiness. The choice is yours. Your family can support you, but they can't choose happiness for you.

6. Caring words are used to communicate, always.

You can measure the happiness of any close relationship by the number of scars that each member carries on their tongues and inner cheeks, formed over many years of biting back angry and insensitive words. Bottom line: Be careful what you say. You can say something unkind in less than one second, but more than a year later the wounds are still there. Don't do this to your family, or anyone for that matter. Every time words are spoken, something is created. Be honest, but also conscious of what you say and how you say it. Use words that lift up, appreciate, encourage, and inspire.

7. Everyone makes *quality* time for each other.

Here's a harsh reality of life: Regardless of the quality of your relationships with your parents, siblings, aunts, uncles, cousins, or close friends, you will miss them when they're gone from your life. And someday they will be.

You have to set aside quality time to share your love openly and honestly with those you love. Realize that no matter how much time you spend with someone you care about, or how much you appreciate them, sometimes it will never seem like you had enough time together. Don't learn this lesson the hard way. Express your love. Tell your family what you need to tell them. Don't shy away from important conversations because you feel awkward or uncomfortable. You never know when you might lose your opportunity.

So stay in close touch with what's going on in your loved ones' lives—communicate openly on a regular basis. Not because it's convenient, but because they are worth the extra effort.

8. Presence is held sacred.

The greatest path to positive influence in any relationship is love. And the greatest path to love is full acceptance within the present moment— allowing everything to be as it is, without hoping or trying to change things.

Presence is recognizing and celebrating that we are all inextricably connected to each other by a power greater than all of us, and that our connection to that power and to one another is grounded in the "now." It's about knowing that you must first attend to the reality of the moment before you can effectively contribute anything positive to it. Practicing presence brings a sense of perspective and purpose to our lives and opens the doorway to loving others as they are.

9. Patience and forgiveness are practiced daily.

No matter how honest and kind you try to be, you will occasionally step on the toes of the people closest to you. And this is precisely why patience and forgiveness are so vital. Patience is the ability to let your light shine on those you love, even after your fuse has blown. And forgiveness is knowing deep down that they didn't mean to blow your fuse in the first place.

Patience and forgiveness can feel bitter at first, but the seeds you plant now will bear sweet fruit in the end.

10 Proven Ways to Raise Smarter, Happier Children

WHEN YOU ASK parents what they want for their children, what are the most common replies? They want their children to be smart and happy, of course.

As parents, we get it. We feel the same way. We're concerned about our son's education and happiness. So we've spent quite a bit of time researching just that—how to raise a smart, happy child. Here's what our extensive research tells us:

1. Walk the talk—always set a great example.

It's not what you say; it's how you live your life every day. Don't tell your children how to live; *live* and let them watch you. Practice what you preach, or don't preach at all. Walk the talk. Your children look up to you, and they will emulate your actions and strive to become who you are.

So *be* who you want them to be.

In other words, be the change you want to see in your child. Give what you expect, reflect what you desire, become what you respect, and mirror what you admire. Every single day.

2. Reduce *your* stress, and thus the stress level in the household.

Not easy, we know, but believe it or not, what children want from their parents more than anything else is for them to be happier and less stressed.

In a survey of a thousand families, researchers asked children, "If you were granted one wish about your parents, what would it be?" Most parents predicted their children would say something about spending more time with them. But they were wrong. The children's number one wish was that their parents would be less tired and less stressed. They wanted their family household to be a less stressful place to live.

Further research has shown that parental stress weakens children's brains, depletes their immune systems, and increases their risk of other unhealthy mental and physical ailments.

3. Believe in your children.

The greatest compliment you can give to a child is to believe in them and let them know you care. When you see something true, good, and beautiful in them, don't hesitate to express your admiration. When you see something that is not true, good, and beautiful in them, don't neglect to give them your wholehearted assistance and guidance.

The simple act of believing that your child is capable and worthy makes a big difference. It gives them confidence and makes them feel qualified to do great things.

In a recent study, elementary school teachers were told that they had certain students in their class who were academically above average. These students were in fact selected at random (they were not necessarily above average in any way). Yet by the end of the school year, 30 percent of the children arbitrarily named as "above average" had gained an average of 22 IQ points, and almost all had gained at least 10 IQ points.

In other words, when the teachers were told certain children were "better," those kids did better in school. When someone you respect believes in you, it helps you be the best you can be. Give your children this opportunity.

4. Praise your children for their effort, not for their intelligence.

Based on the point above, this might sound a bit counterintuitive, but when you praise a child's efforts, you are bringing attention to something they can control—the amount of effort they put in. This is immensely important because it teaches them to persist and that personal growth through hard work is possible. They come to see themselves as in control of their success in life.

In contrast, praising God-given intelligence takes growth and progress out of your child's control, and it provides no good recipe for responding to a failure. Instead of working to improve after setbacks, your child may begin to fear that their innate intelligence just isn't strong enough and then give up rather than lean in.

With that said, a word to the wise: Don't overpraise your kids. Make sure your gestures of praise are warranted. Because if every move your child makes is motivated by a reward like constant praise, when the praise stops, the effort stops too.

The best thing to do? Praise purposefully when it's truly warranted.

And when your child gets stuck, give them a chance to learn that frustrating challenges can be worked through.

5. Don't read *to* your children—read *with* them.

Got a youngster who's learning to read? Don't let them just stare at the pictures in a book while you do all the work by reading every word to them. Instead, call attention to the words. Point to them. Point to the pictures that illustrate them.

Read *with* them, not *to* them.

Research shows this approach helps build a child's reading comprehension. When shared book reading is enriched with explicit attention to the development of a child's reading skills, it truly becomes an effective vehicle for promoting early literacy. Perhaps even more important than that, it makes learning more fun.

6. Eat dinner together as a family.

Eating dinner together makes a difference. Research shows that children who have dinner with their families do better across pretty much every conceivable metric in terms of behavior issues and emotional well-being.

Additional research also suggests that children who enjoy family meals have larger vocabularies, better manners, healthier diets, and higher self-esteem in the long run. The most comprehensive survey done on this topic, a University of Michigan report that examined how American children spent their time, discovered that "the amount of time children spent eating meals at home was the single biggest predictor of better academic achievement and fewer behavioral problems. Mealtime was more influential than time spent in school, studying, attending religious services, or playing sports."

Even if eating dinner together every night isn't possible, try to eat together as a family at least once a week.

7. Create reasonable rules and boundaries for your children.

Children don't do well in a free-for-all environment. It's a myth that being too strict guarantees rebellion and being permissive drives better behavior. From the research we've done, it's clear that children who get in trouble mostly have parents who don't set reasonable rules and boundaries. If their parents are accepting of their behavior no matter what they do, even when they are unruly, children take this lack of rules as a sign that their parents don't really care.

On the flip side, parents who are consistent in enforcing rules and boundaries are often the same parents who become the closest with their children. According to a Penn State study by Dr. Nancy Darling and Dr. Linda Caldwell, parents who set logical rules pertaining to key principles of influence, and explain why the rules are there, engage more closely with the children and ultimately have a happier, healthier relationship with them.

Of course, this doesn't mean you should overdo the rules, or make rules just for the sake of making rules. Parents who are too controlling raise children who are stifled and bored. And stifled, bored kids are likely to rebel.

8. Give your children an opportunity to make healthy peer relationships.

The peer group your children associate with has an enormous effect on their long-term happiness and educational aspirations. As parents, we often think of peer pressure as solely negative, but more often than not, it's positive. Living in a child-friendly neighborhood, going to highly rated schools, and making sure your children associate with the right peers can make a world of difference.

Bottom line: As a human being, you are the average of the people you spend the most time with. And that's why it's not always where you are in life, but who you have by your side that matters most. The same is true for your children.

9. Make sure your children get enough sleep every night.

A tired mind is rarely constructive or content. And it's even worse for children than it is for adults. According to Po Bronson and Ashley Merryman's insightful book, *NurtureShock: New Thinking About Children*, missing an hour of sleep turns a sixth grader's brain into that of a fourth grader. Even a loss of one hour of sleep is equivalent to the loss of two years of cognitive development to the typical child.

There's also a direct correlation between good grades and the average amount of sleep a child gets. Teens who received As average about fifteen more minutes of sleep than B students, who in turn average fifteen more minutes than C students, and so on. Certainly, these are averages, but the research is consistent. For children, every fifteen minutes of sleep counts.

10. Help your children maintain a gratitude journal.

We frequently discuss the powerful benefits of keeping a gratitude journal. And the good news is, it works for children too.

Again, via *NurtureShock*: "In one celebrated example, Dr. Robert Emmons, of the University of California at Davis, asked teenage students to keep a gratitude journal—over ten weeks, the young undergrads listed five things that had happened in the last week which they were thankful for. The results were surprisingly powerful—the students who kept the gratitude journal were 25 percent happier."

Bottom line: Children who keep a gratitude journal are happier, more optimistic, and healthier. As soon as your child is old enough, help them start one.

Afterthoughts

We have learned a lot from the research we've done, but one thing really stands out. It's clear that healthy parenting creates happier children, who are more likely to turn into adults who are better equipped to deal with the realities of life and the worthwhile challenges of nurturing healthy relationships.

40 Things We Need to Teach Our Kids Before They're Too Cool to Hear Our Wisdom

TODAY OUR SON, Mac, started kindergarten. The experience of dropping him off for his very first day of school struck so many emotions for us. As every parent of a school-age child can attest, the very first day of school is a learning experience in and of itself. It's one of those little milestones you anticipate and always remember.

The experience reminds us that there are so many things we want to tell Mac as soon as possible, before he's in high school with his friends and too cool to hear our little nuggets of wisdom—and before we go from "Mommy and Daddy who both know best" to "Mom and Dad who couldn't possibly understand."

So in no particular order, here are forty things we intend to tell him and his little friends, repeatedly, over the next several years:

1. Attitude is a little thing that makes a big difference. Don't base your attitude on how things are. Choose your attitude so it supports and expresses the way you wish them to be. Frustration and stress come from the way you respond and react, not the circumstance itself. Adjust your attitude, and the frustration and stress is gone.

2. What you experience starts with your perception. In almost every case, nothing is stopping you. Nothing is holding you back but your own thoughts about yourself and "how life is." Your perception creates your beliefs. And your beliefs create your behaviors. And your behaviors produce your experience.

3. Let go of the need to complain about life. Spend your moments actually living its beauty. Change the phrase "have to" to "get to." So many things we complain about are things others wish they had the chance to do.

4. Positivity always pays off. Your thoughts do not end when you finish thinking them. They continue to echo through your life. Choose wisely and intentionally. Be outrageously and unreasonably positive. Be funny and creative and ridiculous and joyful all at the same time. Smile as often as possible. A smile actually changes the vibe of your body. It alters, physiologically, the chemistry of your being. It will make you feel better and do better.

5. Negativity just shortens your life. Before you waste it on anger, resentment, spite, or envy, always think of how precious and irreplaceable your time is.

6. Worry is the biggest enemy of the present moment. It does nothing but steal your joy and keep you very busy doing absolutely nothing at all. When you spend time worrying, you're simply using your imagination to create things you don't want.

7. Don't run away from things; run toward them. The best way to move away from something negative is to move toward something positive.

8. Nothing is as bad as it seems. Nothing. There's a benefit and a blessing hidden in the folds of every experience and every outcome.

9. Gratitude helps every situation. How can you transform suffering into joy, and struggle into peace? *Gratitude.* Start being grateful for all the problems you do *not* have.

10. Everything is falling together perfectly, even though it looks as if some things are falling apart. Trust in life's process. Happiness is allowing yourself to be perfectly okay with what is, rather than wishing for and worrying about what is not. When life is "falling apart," things could actually be falling together . . . maybe for the first time.

11. Change is necessary. Change is the process of life itself. In fact, everything is changing every second of our lives. However good or bad the situation is now, it will change. That's one thing you can count on. So never assume that you're stuck with the way things are. Life changes, and so can you. Take a breath of fresh air. The past is long gone. Focus on what you can do, not on what you could have or should have done.

12. You are capable of handling far more than you think. Accept each moment, without judgment or anxiety. Remind yourself that all is well and that you can handle whatever comes along.

13. If you're having problems, that's good. It means you're making progress. The only people with no problems are the ones doing nothing.

14. It takes just as much energy to waste your time as it does to use it wisely. It is far better to be exhausted from lots of effort and learning than to be tired from doing absolutely nothing.

15. There's a big difference between being busy and being productive. Don't confuse motion and progress. A rocking horse keeps moving but never makes any forward progress.

16. You can't achieve what you do not attempt. Everything you achieve comes from something you attempt. Everything! Make the attempt. The path between wanting and having is doing.

17. The right thing and the easy thing are rarely the same thing. Do what matters, not just what is convenient. Do what is fulfilling, not just what is easy. When faced with a choice, choose the path that strengthens you. Choose to learn, choose to grow, choose to more fully become who you are.

18. You can't be your best without first being yourself. Be highly effective by being highly authentic. Take a moment to pause and remember who you are and what you stand for. Take a moment to reflect on the ideas and principles that have real and lasting meaning in your life.

19. Meaningful work is important. You are at your best when you are moving toward a meaningful, positive, and ambitious goal. So never follow goals you're reluctant to pursue. Find ones that will keep you awake at night with excitement.

20. Always realign yourself with your highest priorities. If you're being pulled in every direction by forces beyond your control, take time to realign yourself with what you value most in life. What is important in your life is what you decide is important, and this decision will ultimately create who you are.

21. Set your sights high. Make your dreams big, exciting, and undeniable. They're the ones that will push you forward. Whatever is beyond your reach right now will not always be beyond your reach. Keep going.

22. Miracles happen every day. If we think that miracles are normal, we will expect them. And expecting a miracle is the surest way to get one.

23. If you're going to do something, do it with enthusiasm and devotion. Hold nothing back. In life. Or love. Or business. Or anything at all. Every morning, ask yourself what is really important, and then have the courage to build your day around your answer.

24. Focused effort pays. An attitude of "whatever is convenient" won't accomplish much, ever. An attitude of "whatever it takes" is impossible to stop. So remember, effort does not cost you—it pays. What you invest in effort is never wasted. Sincere, focused effort always brings something of value—an outcome that teaches you what the next step is.

25. What you are capable of achieving is heavily based on how much you want it. When something means enough to you, then you can do it. When you are willing and committed and persistent, you will get yourself there every time.

26. You can always take a small step in the direction of your dreams. There is absolutely nothing about your present situation that prevents you from following your dreams, one step at a time. Use each setback, each disappointment, as a cue to push on ahead with more determination than ever before.

27. Set time aside to celebrate your progress at least once a month. Look at how far you've come. You have made progress. And now, imagine how far you can go.

28. Other people's opinions don't have to be your reality. Let the opinions of others inform you, don't let them limit you. Learn to value yourself and what you stand for. Allow yourself to be yourself. If you don't want what the world says you should want, have the courage to say so.

29. Break the rules sometimes. Don't break the law, but break the rules. If all you are doing is following someone else's rules, then you have not grown—you have only obeyed.

30. You alone get to choose what matters and what doesn't. The meaning of everything in your life is the meaning you give it.

31. Listen to your intuition. When something feels right, that means it is right for you. When something feels wrong, that means it is wrong for you. Pay attention to your authentic feelings, and follow where they lead.

32. Own and embrace your imperfections. Because once you've accepted your flaws, no one can use them against you.

33. Every mistake is a step forward. You cannot make a mistake; you can only make a decision that will be your next best step.

34. Every day is a clean slate. Don't you dare give up on today because of the way things looked yesterday. Don't even think about it. Every day is a new day to try again.

35. No moment is wasted when you live it with presence and purpose. Value and enjoy the journey, even when there are detours along the way. Appreciate every moment, whatever each moment may bring. From the genuine appreciation of these little moments will come a remarkable life.

36. Treat everyone, especially yourself, with kindness and respect. Treat yourself as the most important person in the world, and treat others as you treat yourself. Do not miss a single chance—not one single opportunity—to tell someone how wonderful they are, how beautiful they are inside and out. Live so that people will enjoy your presence when they're with you, and will appreciate you just as much or even more when they're apart from you.

37. Accept important apologies you never receive. If you love someone and you want to forgive them, relieve them of the need to apologize to you, for anything.

38. True love is freedom. Love lets go. Let go of expectation, let go of requirements and rules and regulations that you would impose on your loved ones. The gift of pure love allows you to bless others and accept them without condition, granting them freedom to make their own choices.

39. Everyone you meet can teach you something important. In fact, the people who are the most difficult to deal with can also be your most valuable teachers.

40. No matter how much you know, there's a whole lot you don't know.
In almost every situation, a little more willingness to acknowledge that there may be something you do not know could change everything. Go somewhere new, and countless opportunities suddenly appear. Do something differently, and all sorts of great new possibilities spring up. Keep an open mind.

17 Powerful Truths Every Parent Should Read

It takes courage to raise a child . . .

OUR KIDS CAN'T possibly know what it feels like to be older. And as we age, we forget what it was like to be young.

Spending time with our son helps us tap into our younger mind—he keeps us on our toes. And for that, we are grateful. But we still struggle as parents. We struggle to be present. We struggle to be patient. We struggle to remember. Almost every single day.

Every parent battles with these issues in their own way. Because parenting is not easy.

What helps us is journaling about the lessons parenthood is gradually teaching us, and then referring back to what we've learned when we're struggling and forgetful.

We want to share some quotes from our parenting journal with you. Perhaps they will assist you someday, the way they have assisted us time and time again.

1. Trust yourself. You know far more than you think you do.

2. Parenting is unquestionably one of the hardest things you'll ever do, but in exchange it teaches you about the meaning and power of unconditional love.

3. Everything involving your children will be painful in some way. The emotions are deep, whether they are happiness, heartache, love, or pride. And in the end, they will leave you vulnerable, exposed, and, yes, in pain. The human heart was not meant to beat outside the human body, and yet you will find that your children carry with them just this kind of surreal phenomena—a loving, emotionally attached parent (*you*), with your heart exposed and beating forever outside your chest. Breathe. It's okay.

4. No one is ever quite ready—every parent is caught off guard, again and again. Parenthood chooses you every day, not the other way around. And perhaps a week in, a month in, or even a year in, you open your eyes, look at what you've got, and say, "Oh my goodness"—suddenly awake to the fact that of all the things there ever were to juggle, this is the one you should not drop. It's not a question of choice. It's a presence—of love.

5. The nature of being a parent seems thankless sometimes, until you realize and embrace the fact that you are choosing to love your children far more than you have ever loved anyone before. And you realize, too, that your child can't possibly understand the depth of your love. It's then that you come to understand the tragic, and yet immensely beautiful, unrequited, unconditional love your own parents or certain other individuals have for you.

6. Being a parent is a daily attitude, not a biological relation.

7. To be in your children's memories tomorrow, you have to make time to be in their lives today. Every day of our lives we make deposits in the memory banks of our children. The more present we are, the more deposits we get to make.

8. When you take the time to open your mind and ears, and actually listen, with humility, to what people have to say, it's amazing what you can learn. This is especially true if the people who are doing the talking also happen to be your children.

9. Your children are the greatest gift life will give you, and their souls the heaviest responsibility it will place in your hands. Take time with them, and teach them to have faith in themselves by being a person they can have faith in—a person who listens, a person they can trust without question. When you are old, nothing else you've done will have mattered as much.

10. Walk the talk. Children have never been perfect at listening to their parents, but they have never failed to imitate them in some way.

11. Your children need you to love them for who they are, not spend all your time trying to "fix" them.

12. Children must be taught how to think, not what to think.

13. Parents can only guide by example and put their kids on the right path, but the final forming of a person's character and life story lies in their own hands.

14. If you have never been "hated" by your kid for a short time, you have never truly been a parent. A harsh truth, we know.

15. It's absolutely impossible to protect your children against disappointment in life. Some things you just have to live through to learn.

16. One of the best things you can do for your children as they grow is to let go and allow them to do things for themselves, allow them to be strong and responsible, allow them the freedom to experience things on their own terms, allow them to take the bus or the train and learn from life firsthand—allow them to believe more in themselves and do more by themselves.

17. No matter how great a job you do parenting—especially if you truly do it right—your children won't stay with you. They will eventually break away. It's the one job in life where the better you do, the more surely you won't be needed as often in the long run.

10 Things to Remember About Toxic Family Members

Family is supposed to be our safe haven. Sometimes, however, it's the place where we find the deepest heartache.

LETTING GO OF (or breaking up with) a toxic friend, boyfriend, or girlfriend is one thing, and there's plenty of advice out there for doing so, but what about letting go of a toxic family member?

Most of us are not in a position to just walk away, nor do we feel that we want to, or that it's the right thing to do. So what do we do when a family member is hurting our hearts with their toxicity? How do we deal with our feelings of obligation, confusion, betrayal, and heartache?

First and foremost, you can accept the fact that not everyone's family is healthy or available for them to lean on, to call on, or to go home to. Not every family tie is built on the premise of mutual respect, love, and support. Sometimes "family" simply means that you share a bloodline. That's all. Some family members build us up, and some break us down. So just because someone is blood-related to you doesn't automatically make them the healthiest influence in your life.

Second, you can understand that a toxic family member may be going through a difficult stage in their lives. They may be ill, chronically worried, or lacking what they need in terms of love and emotional support. These people need to be listened to, supported, and cared for (although, whatever the cause of their troubles, you may still need to protect yourself from their toxic behavior at times).

The key thing to keep in mind is that every case of dealing with a toxic family member is a little different, but in any and every case, there are some universal principles we need to remember, for our own sake:

1. They may not be an inherently bad person, but they're not the right person to be spending time with every day.

Not all toxic family relationships are agonizing and uncaring on purpose. Some of them are people who care about you—people who have good intentions but are toxic because their needs and way of existing in the world force you to compromise yourself and your happiness. And as hard as it is, we have to distance ourselves enough to give ourselves space to live. You simply can't hurt yourself on a daily basis for the sake of someone else. You have to make your well-being a priority. Whether that means spending less time with someone, loving a family member from a distance, letting go entirely, or temporarily removing yourself from a situation that feels painful, you have every right to take a step back and create some healthy space for yourself.

2. Toxic people often hide cleverly behind passive aggression.

Passive-aggressive behavior takes many forms but can generally be described as a nonverbal aggression that manifests in negative behavior. Instead of openly expressing how they feel, someone makes subtle, annoying gestures directed at you. Instead of saying what's actually upsetting them, they find small and petty ways to take jabs at you until you pay attention and get upset, sometimes not even realizing why. In a healthy relationship, a loved one won't feel the need to hide behind passive aggression in order to express what they are thinking. So, just be aware of passive aggression when you experience it, and if the other person refuses to reason with you and continues their behavior, you may have no choice but to create some of that space discussed in point number 1.

3. They will try to bully you into submission, if you let them.

We always hear about schoolyard bullies, but the biggest bullies are often toxic family members. And bullying is never okay. Period! There is no freedom on earth that gives someone the right to assault who you are as a person. Sadly, some people just won't be happy until they've pushed your ego to the ground and stomped on it. What you might have to do is have the nerve to stand up for yourself. Don't give them leeway. Nobody has the power to make you feel small unless you give them that power. It takes a great deal of courage to stand up to your enemies, but just as much to stand up to your family and friends. Sometimes bullying comes from the most unlikely places. Be cognizant of how the people closest to you treat you, and look out for the subtle jabs they throw. When necessary, confront them—do whatever it takes to give yourself the opportunity to grow into who you really are.

4. Pretending their toxic behavior is okay is not okay.

If you're not careful, toxic family members can use their moody behavior to get preferential treatment, because, well, it just seems easier to quiet them down than to listen to their rhetoric. Don't be fooled. Short-term ease equals long-term pain for you in a situation like this. Toxic people don't change if they are being rewarded for not changing. Decide this minute not to be influenced by their behavior. Stop tiptoeing around them or making special pardons for their continued belligerence. Constant drama and negativity is never worth putting up with. If someone in your family over the age of twenty-one can't be a reasonable, reliable, respectful adult on a regular basis, it's time to remove yourself from the line of fire.

5. You do not have to neglect yourself just because they do.

Practice self-care every day. Seriously, if you're forced to live with a toxic person, then make sure you get enough alone time to rest and recuperate. Having to play the role of a focused, rational adult in the face of toxic moodiness can be exhausting, and if you're not careful, the toxicity can infect you. Toxic family members can keep you up at night as you constantly question yourself: "Am I doing the right thing? Am I really so terrible that they despise me so much? I can't *believe* she did that! I'm so hurt!" Thoughts like these can agonize you for weeks, months, or even years. Sometimes this is the goal of a toxic family member: to drive you mad and make you out to be the crazy one. Because oftentimes they have no idea why they feel the way they do, and they can't see beyond their own emotional needs, hence their relentless toxic communication and actions. And since you can't control what they do, it's important to take care of yourself so that you can remain centered, feeling healthy, and ready to live positively in the face of negativity when you must—mindfulness, meditation, prayer, and regular exercise work wonders!

6. If their toxic behavior becomes physical, it's a legal matter that must be addressed.

If you've survived the wrath of a physical abuser in your family, and you tried to reconcile things . . . if you forgave, and you struggled, and even if the expression of your grief had you succumb to outbursts of toxic anger . . . if you spent years hanging on to the notions of trust and faith, even after you knew in your heart that those beautiful intangibles, upon which love is built and sustained, would never be returned . . . and especially if you stood up as the barrier between an abuser and someone else, and took the brunt of the abuse in their place—you are a *hero*! But now it's time to be the hero of your future. Enough is enough! If someone is physically abusive, they are breaking the law, and they need to deal with the consequences of their actions.

7. Although it's hard, you can't take their toxic behavior personally.

When a person is being obviously toxic, it's them, not you. *Know* this. Toxic family members will likely try to imply that somehow you've done something wrong. And because the feeling-guilty button is quite large on many of us, even the implication that we might have done something wrong can hurt our confidence and unsettle our resolve. Don't let this happen to you. Remember, there is a huge amount of freedom that comes to you when you take nothing personally. Most toxic people behave negatively not just to you but to everyone they interact with. Even when the situation seems personal—even if you feel directly insulted—it usually has nothing to do with you. What they say and do, and the opinions they have, are based heavily on their own self-reflection—their feelings and understandings about life.

8. Hating them for being toxic only brings more toxicity into your life.

As the saying attributed to Gandhi goes, "An eye for an eye will only make the whole world blind." Regardless of how despicable a family member has acted, never let hate build in your heart. Fighting hatred with hatred only hurts you more. When you decide to hate someone, you automatically begin digging two graves: one for your enemy and one for yourself. Hateful grudges are for those who insist that they are owed something. Forgiveness, on the other hand, is for those who are strong enough and smart enough to move on. After all, the best revenge is to be unlike the person who hurt you. The best revenge is living well, in a way that creates peace in your heart.

9. People can change, and some toxic family relationships can be repaired in the long run.

When trust is broken, which happens in nearly every family relationship at some point, it's essential to understand that it can be repaired, provided both people are willing to do the hard work of self-growth. In fact, it's at this time, when it feels like the solid bedrock of your relationship has crumbled into dust, that you're being given an opportunity to shed the patterns and dynamics with each other that haven't been serving you. It's painful work and a painful time, and the impulse will be to walk away, especially if you believe that broken trust cannot be repaired. But if you understand that trust levels rise and fall over the course of a lifetime, you'll be more likely to find the strength to hang in, hang on, and grow together. But it does take two. You can't do it alone.

10. Sadly, sometimes all you can do is let go for good.

All details aside, this is your life. You may not be able to control all the things toxic family members do to you, but you can decide not to be reduced by them in the long run. You can decide not to let their actions and opinions continuously invade your heart and mind. And above all, you can decide whom to walk beside tomorrow, and whom to leave behind today. In a perfect world we would always be able to fix our relationships with toxic family members, but as we all know, the world isn't perfect. Put in the effort and do what you can to keep things intact, but don't be afraid to let go and do what's right for *you* when you must.

CHILDREN & FAMILY QUESTIONS
TO MAKE *YOU* THINK

What can parents do to raise smart, happy children?

What has personal experience taught you?

What do you want to tell your kids before they're "too cool" to hear your wisdom?

What reminders, quotes, or rituals help you when you're struggling to be a good mom or dad?

Are there any specific habits or actions that have made you and your children happier as a family?

What's one question you need to start asking more often of the people you love?

Can you think of a time when taking a deep breath and practicing some mindful reflection saved you from overreacting and responding to someone inappropriately?

What do you truly value in life?

What's one frequent distraction that wastes your time and gets between you and your relationships?

What stressful burdens do you need to let go of and rise above?

PART FOUR

Friendships & Everyday Relationships

Open Yourself to Others

THE SOCIAL RELATIONSHIPS that we have built over the years have been quite intentional. We have friends of all different backgrounds, demographics, and religions. And the experience of interacting with someone outside your normal circle, who doesn't live on your block or share the same upbringing, is such a beautiful thing and can be truly eye-opening. On one hand, there's a lot of differences between us that we can learn from. But on other hand, it also shows us how similar we really are. Ultimately we want a lot of the same things: peace in our lives, a sense of community, little slices of joy, simple pleasures, and a feeling of making progress. Not all these people live right next door to us, and yet all of them have added value to our lives, and it's something we're truly grateful for.

Unfortunately, we know how easily relationships with friends and colleagues are pushed aside and put on the back burner. And yet we all need to have great relationships in our lives, outside our immediate family and intimate circle, so it is important to dedicate time to nurture those relationships.

How do we do that?

Sometimes it can be as simple as shooting a video text to say, "Hi. How are you? What's going on?" Jumping on a FaceTime or Zoom call and seeing a friend can make a world of difference—to truly see each other, to truly recognize and appreciate the unique person you care about. It doesn't have to be every single day, by any means. Angel has been friends with her best friend since she was five years old, and they get together or FaceTime for an hour once a month. That may not sound like much, but they always pick up right where they left off. You can have relationships with friends you don't need to see or talk to every day, but you do find ways to nurture that friendship and stay in touch, whatever that looks like for you.

Other times, we look for ways to schedule time and create rituals to nurture friendships. For Angel, if it's not on the calendar, it's not going to happen, so she turns meetups with friends into a ritual. For example, our son, Mac, made a friend named Leo at day care, but now they go to different schools. So Angel and Mac meet Leo and his mom at the beach every Thursday after school, like clockwork. It's something that happens every week; Angel doesn't even have to think about it, and it helps her to know that's what they're doing without worrying about shuffling things around to make it happen.

Here's another example of rituals with friends: When Marc worked at his former job, he and some colleagues would take a long walk together after lunch. It was a daily ritual to take thirty minutes to talk while they walked outside around the office park. These relationships were nurtured on a daily basis, and Marc became great friends with those guys—he was even in two of their weddings.

Friendships are incredible drivers of happiness. So today, think of little rituals you can build into your life to help nurture relationships with people and open yourself up to others.

10 Types of Friends Worth Fighting For

THIS CHAPTER WAS inspired by three emails we've received, all of which share a similar theme about friendship. Below we have shared a small excerpt from each (with permission). We know you will appreciate them:

- "Kayla, my 12-year-old daughter, speaks fluent sign language because her best friend, Megan, whom she grew up with from the time she was an infant, is deaf. Seeing their genuine friendship evolve and grow over the years truly warms my heart."
- "My younger brother, Greg, spends most of his free time at school hanging out with the football team—he's actually been working out with the team and everything. Greg has a mild case of autism. About a year ago my mom was ready to pull him out of school and have him homeschooled due to excessive bullying from peers. One of the popular football players, who had stood up for him in the past, heard about this, explained the situation to his teammates and friends, and stood by his side until the bullying stopped. Now, a year later, he's just 'one of the guys.'"

- "Yesterday my sister and I were in a pretty bad car accident. Luckily both of us were wearing our seat belts and didn't have any major injuries. My sister is and always has been Ms. Popular—she knows everyone. I'm the complete opposite—an introvert who hangs out with the same two girls all the time. My sister immediately posted a comment on Facebook and Instagram about our accident. And while all her friends were commenting, my two friends showed up independently at the scene of the accident before the ambulance arrived."

Each of these emails made us smile because they reminded us of the power of true friendship. There's honestly nothing more beautiful and meaningful in this world.

The author of the third email excerpt above ended her email with this line: "I know I don't have a lot of friends, but I'm sure grateful I have a couple worth fighting for."

And that's exactly what we want to reflect on here—ten types of friends worth fighting for:

1. Friends who make time for each other

There are countless intricacies to every great friendship, but the foundation is always incredibly simple: making time for each other. The key is to hang in, stay connected, fight for them, and let them fight for you. Don't walk away when the going gets a little tough, don't be distracted too easily, don't be too busy or tired, and don't take them for granted. Friends are part of the glue that holds life and happiness together. It's powerful stuff!

So put down the smartphone, close the laptop, and enjoy each other's company, face-to-face, the old-fashioned way.

There are few joys that equal a good conversation, a genuine laugh, a long walk, a friendly dance, or a big hug shared by two people who care about each other. Sometimes the most ordinary things can be made extraordinary simply by doing them with the right people. You know this! Choose to be around these people, and choose to make the most of your time together.

2. Friends who are willing to put in the necessary effort

Healthy, long-term friendships are amazing, but rarely easygoing 24/7. Why? Because they require flexibility and compromise.

Two different people will always have two slightly different perspectives about the same situation. Resisting this truth and seeing the hard times as immediate evidence that something is catastrophically wrong, or that you're supposed to see eye-to-eye on everything, only aggravates the difficulties. By contrast, finding the willingness to view the challenges as learning opportunities will give you the energy and strength you need to continue to move forward and grow your friendship for decades to come.

3. Friends who believe in each other

Sometimes we see our worst selves, our most vulnerable and weak selves. We need someone else to get close enough to tell us we're wrong. Someone we trust. That's what true friends are for.

Simply believing in another person, and showing it in words and deeds on a consistent basis, can make a *huge* difference in their life. Several studies of people who grew up in dysfunctional homes, but who grew up to be happy and successful, show that the one thing they had in common was someone who believed in them. Be this someone for those you care about. Support their dreams. Participate with them.

Cheer for them. Be nothing but encouraging. Whether they actually follow through with their present dreams, or completely change their minds, is irrelevant; your belief in them is of infinite importance, either way.

4. Friends who face challenges and weaknesses together

When we honestly ask ourselves which friends have helped us the most, we often find that it's those special few who, instead of giving lots of advice, specific solutions, or quick cures, have chosen rather to share in our challenges and touch our wounds with a listening ear and a loving heart.

The friend who can be silent with us in a moment of confusion, who can stay with us in an hour of pain and mourning, who can tolerate not knowing or having all the answers, not curing and fixing everything in an instant, but instead simply facing the reality of our momentary powerlessness with us—that is a friend worth fighting for.

5. Friends who are gentle and compassionate through life's changes

Be gentle and compassionate with your friends as they evolve and change. Mother Nature opens millions of flowers every day without forcing the buds. Let this be a reminder not to be forceful with those you care about, but to simply give them enough light and love, and an opportunity to grow naturally.

Ultimately, how far you go in life depends on your willingness to be helpful to the young, respectful to the aged, tender with the hurt, supportive of the striving, and tolerant of those who are weaker or stronger than the majority. Because we wear many hats throughout the course of our lives, at some point in your life you will have been all of these people, and the same is true for your friends.

6. Friends who support each other's growth

No human being is your friend who demands your silence or denies your right to grow.

Healthy friendships always move in the direction of personal growth: for the relationship as a whole and for each individual in it. A desire to impede the growth of the other for one's personal comfort is an expression of fear.

When you connect with a true friend, this person helps you find the best in yourself. In this way, neither of you actually meet the best in each other; you both grow into your best selves by spending time together and nurturing each other's growth.

7. Friends who tell the truth

Subconsciously, many of us prefer gentle lies to hard truths.

Don't do this. Don't hide behind lies. Deal with the truth, learn the lessons, endure the consequences of reality, and move your friendship forward.

8. Friends who are tolerant of each other's inevitable mood swings

Giving your friends the space to save face and not taking things personally when they're occasionally upset, cranky, or having a bad day is a priceless gift.

Truth be told, what others say and do is often based entirely on their own self-reflection. When a friend who is angry and upset speaks to you, and you nevertheless remain present and continue to treat them with kindness and respect, you place yourself in a position of great power. You become a means for the situation to be graciously diffused and healed.

9. Friends who work out their issues with each other, not with others

This is something we have already discussed, but it's worth mentioning again: *Never* post negatively about a friend on social media. Fourteen-year-old schoolkids post negatively about their friends on social media. It's a catty way to get attention and vent, when the emotionally healthy response is to talk your grievances over with them directly when the time is right.

Don't fall into the trap of getting others on your side either, because healthy friendships only have one side—it's called mutual respect.

Furthermore, friendships and their intricacies don't always make sense, especially from the outside. So don't let outsiders run your friendship for you. If you're having an issue with a friend, work it out with *them* and no one else.

10. Friends who are faithful from a distance

Sometimes life puts geographic barriers between you and a good friend. But growing apart geographically doesn't change the fact that for a long time you two grew side by side; your roots will always be tangled. Knowing this, embracing it, and making the best of it . . . that's a clear sign of true friendship.

In the end, this true kind of friendship is a promise made in the heart—silent, unwritten, unbreakable by distance, and unchangeable by time.

40 Things We Forget to Thank Our Best Friends For

I don't need a certain number of friends,
just a number of friends I can be certain of.

SOME OF OUR best friends are family, some we've known since we were kids, and others are newer friendships that continue to grow stronger by the day. Although they are all very different, every one of them is extraordinary. We wouldn't be who we are today without these people in our lives. And despite the fact that we know this, we often take our best friends for granted. We forget to thank them, for almost everything. So here's our attempt at setting the record straight:

1. **"Thank you for making so many ordinary moments extraordinary."** Yes, sometimes the most ordinary things can be made extraordinary, just by doing them with the right people.

2. **"Thank you for always giving me the extra push I need."** A best friend is someone who will inspire you to be who you always knew you could be. Keep this in mind. Anyone who helps you make your

half-hearted attempts more wholehearted through kindness, commitment, and teamwork, is a keeper.

3. **"Thank you for telling me the truth."** Remember, being honest might not always get you a lot of friends, but it will always get you the right ones. Too many of us prefer gentle lies to hard truths.

4. **"Thank you for talking things out with me."** Lots of problems in the world would disappear if we talked to each other instead of about each other. So always communicate clearly with those closest to you, even when it's uncomfortable and uneasy.

5. **"Thank you for meeting me halfway."** Best friends ultimately meet in the middle. When there's a disagreement, they figure out a solution that works for both parties—a compromise, rather than a need for the other person to change or completely give in.

6. **"Thank you for not getting in the way of the other important parts of my life."** A healthy relationship will never require you to sacrifice your happiness, your other important relationships, your dreams, or your dignity.

7. **"Thank you for being compassionate."** Let their kindness and compassion remind you to pay it forward. Always give those around you the break that you hope the world will give you on your own bad day, and you will never, ever regret it.

8. **"Thank you for thinking of me as often as you do."** Make little gestures daily to show your best friends you care. Knowing that a person you often think of has you on their mind too means a lot.

9. "Thank you for the compliments." It's nice to be complimented, isn't it? Do not miss a chance—not one single, tiny opportunity—to tell someone you care about how wonderful they are and how beautiful they are, inside and out.

10. "Thank you for making time for me." When you are important to another person, they will always find a way to make time for you—no excuses, no lies, and no broken promises.

11. "Thank you for your full presence." The best gift you can give someone you care about is the purity of your full attention. That's what best friends do for each other every time they're together.

12. "Thank you for knowing when something is wrong with me." An incredible thing happens when we pay close attention to each other. We help each other heal, sometimes before we even hurt. A person who truly knows and loves you—a best friend—is someone who sees the pain in your eyes while everyone else still believes the smile on your face.

13. "Thank you for making the extra effort to understand me." It's much easier to judge people than it is to understand them; understanding takes extra kindness and patience. And this "extra" is always worth it.

14. "Thank you for not acting, judging, or treating me like you know me better than I know myself." Enough said.

15. "Thank you for being willing to be wrong." Sometimes we must choose to be wrong, not because we really are wrong, but because we value our relationship more than our pride.

16. "Thank you for supporting my decisions." Don't listen to those who tell you exactly what to do. Listen to those special few who encourage you to do what you already know in your heart is right.

17. "Thank you for being loyal, even when we are apart." Best friends don't grow apart, even when they are apart.

18. "Thank you for being there through good times and bad." The people who stick by you at your worst deserve to enjoy being with you at your best. In fact, the best thing about the toughest days of your life is that you get to see who your true friends really are. The people truly worthy of "best friend" status are the ones who help you through hard times, and laugh with you after the hard times pass.

19. "Thank you for knowing that I can't always be strong." Sometimes we must let a friend down because we can't hold them up. But "I can't carry you" doesn't mean "I don't love you." It may simply mean "I'm struggling too."

20. "Thank you for facing problems with me." Best friends are those who make your problems their problems too, just so you don't have to go through them alone. Don't look for someone who will solve all your problems; look for someone who will face them with you.

21. "Thank you for going out of your way for me, even when it's not convenient." You never want to waste your time with someone who wants you around only when it's convenient for them. Because that's not what true friendship is all about.

22. "Thank you for actually wanting to be there for me." True friendship is never burdened with stressful promises and obligations. What best friends do for each other should be done because they care and because they want to do them. Period.

23. "Thank you for walking the talk." When we characterize people by their actions, we are never fooled by their words. Best friends don't just talk the talk; they walk it out.

24. "Thank you for believing in me." It's amazing how far you are willing to go when someone believes in you.

25. "Thank you for encouraging me when I stumble." Return the favor when you're able. We have enough critics. Be an encourager. One sincere word of encouragement after failure is worth more than a day of praise after success. Be a blessing. Be a friend. Encourage someone special. Take time to care. Let your words heal and not wound.

26. "Thank you for using caring words." You never know what someone is going through on any given day. Kindness and compassion are always welcome.

27. "Thank you for accepting me just the way I am." A best friend is someone who truly knows you, and loves you just the same. Don't change so people will like you. Be yourself, and the right people will love the real you.

28. "Thank you for making me feel comfortable in my skin." This is such an important reminder. Be the type of person who makes everyone you come across feel perfectly okay and comfortable with being exactly who they are.

29. "Thank you for simply enjoying my company." Lots of relationships fail because we spend more time pointing out each other's mistakes and not enough time enjoying each other's company.

30. "Thank you for valuing my time." Anyone who is best-friend material will value your time. Period. Never waste your time on someone who doesn't value it.

31. "Thank you for showing me that you are grateful to have me in your life." Showing gratitude is one of the simplest yet most powerful things humans can do for each other.

32. "Thank you for supporting me in making myself a priority." Remember, putting yourself first does not mean being "selfish"—it means being self-aware. It means not forgetting to love yourself too.

33. "Thank you for sincerely loving me." Nothing changes the world for the better like one person deciding to love another, no matter what. Today, invest your love in someone special, and thank those special friends who invest their love in you.

34. "Thank you for helping me love myself more too." What you give to another person is really what you give to yourself. When you treat people you care about with love, you learn that you're lovable too.

35. "Thank you for all the little things you do that make a big difference." Pay attention to the little things, because when you really miss someone, you miss the little things the most—like just laughing together.

36. "Thank you for being patient and forgiving when I step on your toes." Remind yourself again: No matter how honest and kind you try to be, you will occasionally step on the toes of the people closest to you. And this is precisely why patience and forgiveness are so vital. Patience is the ability to let your light shine on those you love, even after your fuse has blown. And forgiveness is knowing deep down that they didn't mean to blow your fuse in the first place.

37. "Thank you for not holding my unchangeable past against me." Sometimes happiness in relationships amounts to making peace with something that can't be fixed. Sometimes you let it go, and sometimes you hold it broken. It amounts to forgiveness in any case.

38. "Thank you for not expecting our relationship to always be easy." Healthy relationships don't just happen; they take time, patience, and two people who truly want to work together to create something meaningful and lasting.

39. "Thank you for giving me the solitude and space I need." Remember, it's healthy to spend time alone sometimes. You need to know how to be alone and not be defined by another person.

40. "And most of all, thank you for being *you*."

10 Relationship Tips Everyone Forgets

SEVERAL YEARS AGO, on their fiftieth wedding anniversary, Marc's eighty-seven-year-old grandfather looked at his eighty-four-year-old grandmother and said, "This right here, our relationship, this is my greatest accomplishment. You are my best friend!"

Those words have always remained with both of us, and especially with Marc. They were beautifully romantic, but more importantly, they were delightfully true. Healthy relationships and friendships are accomplishments. They take commitment and work, and two people who are willing to meet in the middle and put in the necessary effort.

If you're in a relationship that could use a little help, whether intimate or a platonic friendship, the tips below will come in handy.

1. Let go of old wounds through forgiveness.

Every moment of your life you are either growing or dying—and when you are physically healthy, it's a choice, not fate. The art of maintaining happiness in your life and relationships relies on the fine balancing act of holding on and letting go. Yes, sometimes people you trust (including yourself) will hurt you. Being hurt is something you can't avoid, but being continuously miserable is always a choice. Forgiveness is the remedy. You have to let go of what's behind you before you can grasp the goodness in front of you.

2. Come clean when you make a mistake.

An honest heart is the beginning of everything that is right with this world. The most honorable people of all are not those who never make mistakes, but rather those who admit to their mistakes, and then go on and do their best to right their wrongs. In the end, being honest might not always win you a lot of friends and lovers, but it will always keep the right ones in your life.

3. Stop gossiping and start communicating.

A good rule of thumb: If you can't say it to their face, you shouldn't say it behind their back. As Eleanor Roosevelt once said, "Great minds discuss ideas, average minds discuss events, and small minds discuss people." Life is much too short to waste talking about people, gossiping, and stirring up trouble that has no substance. If you don't know, ask. If you don't agree, say so. If you don't like it, speak up. But never judge people behind their back.

4. Give others the space to make their own decisions.

Stop judging others by your own past. Never act, judge, or treat people like you know them better than they know themselves. They are living a different life from yours. What might be good for one person may not be good for another. What might be bad for one person might change another person's life for the better. Allow the people in your life to make their own mistakes and their own decisions.

5. Do things that make *you* happy.

If you want to awaken happiness in a relationship, start by living a life that makes you happy and then radiate your happiness into your relationship. If you want to eliminate suffering in a relationship, start by eliminating the dark and negative parts of yourself, and then radiate your positivity into your relationship. Truly, the greatest power you have in this world is the power of your own self-transformation. All the positive change you seek in any relationship starts with the one in the mirror.

6. Show your loved ones your kindness in small ways every day.

No act of kindness, however small, is ever wasted. Nothing could be closer to the truth. Always be kinder than necessary. You never know what someone is going through. Sometimes you have to be kind to someone, not because they're being nice, but because you are. Too often we underestimate the power of a touch, a smile, a kind word, a listening ear, an honest compliment, or the smallest act of caring, all of which have the potential to turn a life around.

7. Say less when less means more.

It takes some courage to stand up and speak; it takes even more courage to open your mind and listen. Pay attention and be a good listener. Your ears will never get you in trouble. The people in your life often need a listening ear more than they need a rambling voice. And don't listen with the intent to reply; hear what is being said with the intent to understand. You are as beautiful as the love you give, and you are as wise as the silence you leave behind.

8. Let your love and trust overpower your fear.

You never lose by loving; you lose by holding back. No relationship is impossible until you refuse to give it a chance. Love means giving someone the chance to hurt you but trusting them not to. Without this trust, a relationship cannot survive. You can't live in fear of others hurting you; you have to believe in the good faith of others. If you are ever going to have someone trust you, you must feel that you can trust them too.

9. Accept, don't expect.

Unconditional acceptance is something we want but rarely ever give out. Remember, people never do anything that is out of character. They may do things that go against your expectations, but what people do reveals exactly who they are. Never force your expectations on people, other than the expectation that they will be exactly who they are. Who they are is not what they say or what you have come to expect; it is who they reveal themselves to be. Either you accept them as they are, or you move on without them.

10. Let the wrong ones go.

Know your worth! When you give your time to someone who doesn't respect you, you surrender pieces of your heart you will never get back. All failed relationships hurt, but losing someone who doesn't appreciate and respect you is actually a gain, not a loss. Some people come into your life temporarily simply to teach you something. They come and they go, and they make a difference. It's perfectly okay that they're not in your life anymore. You now have more time to focus on the relationships that truly matter.

Afterthoughts

Remember, even the healthiest relationships have small flaws. Being too black and white about the quality and health of a relationship spells trouble. Accept the fact that there will always be difficulties present, but you can still focus on the good. Instead of constantly looking for signs of what's not working in your relationship, what you need to look for are signs of what is working, and then use that as a solid foundation to build on.

28 Ways to Uncomplicate Your Relationships

ALMOST TWO DECADES ago, when Marc asked his grandfather for some relationship advice, he said, "Honestly, the moment I stopped trying to find the right woman and started trying to become the right man, your grandmother walked up to me and said, 'Hello.'"

This small tip immediately changed the way Marc treated himself and others. In fact, it set the foundation for all the healthy relationships he's nurtured over the years, including our marriage.

The bottom line is that every single one of our relationships starts within us. When we uncomplicate ourselves, we uncomplicate our interactions with others. When we stop doing the wrong things and start doing the right things, our relationships get a lot easier.

Which means it's time to . . .

1. Stop looking to others for the love and respect only you can give yourself. Self-respect, self-worth, and self-love—there's a reason they all start with "self." You can't receive them from anyone else.

2. Start accepting and embracing your flaws. Once you've accepted your flaws, no one can use them against you. Love yourself! Forgive yourself! Accept yourself! You are *you*, and that's the beginning and the end. No apologies, no regrets.

3. Stop comparing and competing every second. Take one step at a time and don't compare your progress with that of others. We all need our own time to travel our own distance. Remember this, and give others the space to do the same.

4. Start letting others be exactly who they are. Remember, a great relationship is about two things: First, appreciating the similarities; and second, respecting the differences.

5. Stop being insensitive. Always be kinder than you feel. Yes, be *waaaay* kinder than necessary. You never know what someone is going through. If you cannot speak a kind word, say nothing at all.

6. Start showing your love. Don't just say it; let your actions speak too. Showing someone you care is wonderful, and it's easy. Sometimes the smallest act of love can take up the greatest space in someone's heart. To make someone happy, give them three things: attention, affection, and appreciation.

7. Stop judging. The more you judge, the less you see and love. It's easy to look at people and make quick judgments about them—their present and their past—but you'd be amazed at the pain and tears a single smile hides. What a person shows to the world is only one tiny tip of the iceberg hidden from sight. And more often than not, it's lined with cracks and scars that go all the way to the foundation of their soul. Never judge; learn to respect and acknowledge the feelings of another.

8. Start acting like what you do makes a difference. You are needed. You matter. Always go above and beyond for those who need you most. In a world full of people who couldn't care less, be someone who couldn't care more.

9. Stop letting one dark cloud obliterate the whole sky. Don't sweat the small stuff today. Don't let stupid little daily frustrations interfere with your relationships. Just do the best you can. Live simply. Love generously. Speak honestly. Work diligently. Then let go and let what's meant to be, *be*.

10. Start doing what's right for *you* too. Remember, if you care too much about what other people think, in a way you will always be their prisoner. You can't live your entire life for someone else. Sometimes you've got to do what's right for you, even if someone you care about disagrees.

11. Stop needing to always be right. Sometimes we must choose to be wrong, not because we really are wrong, but because we value our relationship more than our pride.

12. Start asking yourself, "Will this hurt someone I care about in any way?" The bottom line is that you can't keep hurting someone over and over and expect them to love and respect you.

13. Stop focusing on outer beauty all the time. Focus on inner beauty. In the end, people are not as beautiful as they look, walk, or talk. They are only as beautiful as they love, as they care, and as they share. Also, a little formula to keep in mind for yourself: Self + Confident + Honesty = Beautiful.

14. Start noticing the little things. Pay extra close attention to those you care about. It's nice when a friend remembers every tiny detail about you. Not because you keep reminding them, but because they pay attention and care.

15. Stop pressuring others into things, or putting up with those who pressure you. Be patient. Let people decide for themselves. Being willing to wait is a sign of true love and friendship. Anyone can say that they care about you, but not everyone will wait for you.

16. Start using your voice to lift others up. Let your voice inspire people every day, so much that they think to themselves, "I'm so lucky to have such a good life." Let your voice be the thing that lights a fire in others and keeps them going even when it hurts. Let your voice be the one they hear in their dreams that tells them, "You are so loved, you are so wanted, you are a special gift, and you are worthy."

17. Stop taking things personally. Whatever happens in a relationship, however people behave, just don't take things too personally. Nothing other people do is because of you; it's because of them. Their actions are a direct result of *their* thoughts, feelings, and emotions.

18. Start letting honest mistakes slide. Lots of relationships fail because we spend more time pointing out each other's mistakes and not enough time enjoying each other's company. So remember that *everyone* makes mistakes. If you can't forgive others, don't expect others to forgive you.

19. Stop being dramatic. Spend less time gossiping about problems and more time helping yourself and others solve them. Stay out of people's needless drama and don't create your own.

20. Start forgiving yourself for the pain you caused in the past. People can be more forgiving than you can imagine, but you have to forgive yourself too. Let go of what's bitter and move on.

21. Stop letting your expectations get in the way of your love. Love is simply friendship without unjust expectations. It is a quiet understanding, a mutual confidence, and a commitment to sharing and forgiving. It is loyalty through good and bad times. It settles for less than perfection and makes allowances for human weaknesses.

22. Start being honest about how you feel. Remember, being honest might not always get you a lot of friends, but it will always get you the right ones.

23. Stop spending time with those who continuously belittle you. Don't let anyone make you feel that you don't deserve the good things happening in your life. You deserve to be happy. You deserve to live a life you are excited about. Don't let anyone make you forget that. Surround yourself with people who make you a better person—those who inspire you to be your best self.

24. Start giving yourself all the approval you need. Say it: "I am who I am, and your approval isn't needed." Just be yourself and let the right people love the real you. Find people who respect you as much as you respect them. Be with those who are happy and proud to have you just the way you are.

25. Stop saying yes when you want to say no. You can't always be agreeable; that's how people take advantage of you. Sometimes you have to set clear boundaries.

26. Start communicating clearly. Don't try to read other people's minds, and don't make other people try to read yours. Most problems, big and small, within a family, friendship, or business relationship, start with bad communication. Someone isn't being clear.

27. Stop making it all about *you*. The most successful people in the most successful relationships are looking for ways to help others. The most unsuccessful people are still asking, "What's in it for me?"

28. Start living with 100 percent integrity. Don't cheat. Be faithful. Be kind. Do the right thing! It is a less complicated way to live. Integrity is the essence of everything successful. When you break the rules of integrity, you invite serious complications into your life. Keep life simple and enjoyable by doing what you know in your heart is right.

And finally, remember that good relationships don't just happen; they take time, patience, commitment, and two people who truly want to work to be together.

5 Powerful Rituals for Meeting the Right People & Building New, Healthy Relationships

WE HAD A recent conversation with our friend Thanh about the importance of establishing healthy, positive, supportive relationships. This is a topic that fascinates us, and it's something we know a lot about.

We met Thanh at a business conference in Las Vegas some years back. We hit it off as friends almost immediately—there was lots of synergy between our interests in personal development and in expanding our entrepreneurial business ventures.

But the kicker is the immense (and immediate) positive impact Thanh's friendship has had on both our personal and professional growth. The undeniable truth became crystal clear to us rather quickly: Who you associate with makes all the difference in your life. Positive relationships form the foundation of a happy, rewarding life.

If your time and energy is misspent on the wrong relationships, or on too many activities that force you to neglect your good relationships, you can end up in a tedious cycle of fleeting friendships, superficial romances that are as thrilling as they are meaningless, and a general sense of wondering why you always seem to be running in place, chasing affection.

In many ways, we, as human beings, are like koi fish. The koi fish grows in proportion to its environment. If you keep it in a small bucket of water, it grows to only a few inches in length. But if you let it loose in the wild, it can grow up to two feet long. Are you like the koi fish that has been kept in a small bucket? Is your environment and social network stifling your personal and professional growth? If so, how do you make changes and build healthier relationships?

So how do you build healthy, lasting relationships? How do you find friends who lift you higher? How do you meet a significant other who belongs at your family reunions? How do you meet the right people?

During our conversation with Thanh, all three of us agreed that it's not hard to build and nurture healthy relationships as long as you are willing to uphold five essential rituals for doing so:

1. Learn to enjoy your own company.

Ironically, the prerequisite for building healthy relationships is being comfortable when you're all by yourself. If you're starting fresh, with a minimal number of friends in your immediate vicinity, the reason for this is obvious: Spending time alone is your only option. Likewise, if you have friends who have been dragging you down and negatively impacting your life, withdrawing from them and starting anew will likely require a bit more alone time.

Appreciating solitude starts with the conscious awareness of the freedom it brings. When you enjoy your own company, you don't need others around for the sake of having others around. You can be flexible about who you choose to spend time with, instead of letting your fear of being alone suck you into social situations and relationships that aren't right for you.

It's also important to note that being desperate for the company of others will hinder your ability to authentically interact and communicate. You'll be more worried about achieving external validation instead of just letting your truth flow and being open to establishing honest human connections.

With that said, however, journeying through life on your own two feet is a learning process—you become stronger as you go. It's like a kid who can't find her way home when she's alone: doing it the first few times is daunting and scary, but in the long run she's safer and better off having learned the way.

So just remember, it's always better to learn to stand on your own two feet and walk alone when you must, rather than to have someone carry you around your whole life. And once you are reasonably self-sufficient, then relying on someone else from time to time is an act of inner strength, not weakness.

Try to spend some time alone every day on a solo project that interests you—reading, writing, painting, coding, etc. The goals is to get to the point where you are just as happy staying in as going out, as long as you keep a healthy balance between the two.

2. Get in touch.

A big part of meeting the right people is reacquainting yourself with the good people you already know. It's all about initiating friendly interactions, instead of waiting for others to make the first move. We bet you can think of several people that you have been terrible at keeping in touch with. These might be extended family members, old college friends, previous coworkers you enjoyed spending time with, or even current friends you rarely talk to.

Dig back into your past and make a list of people you wish you had stayed in better touch with. Then contact them. An email or a text message might work best to break the ice if you're contacting someone you haven't talked to in a while. If you have lost a person's contact information, Google them, or look them up on Facebook, Twitter, LinkedIn, Instagram, etc. Or perhaps you have a mutual friend or acquaintance who can put you back in touch.

This practice might sound overly simple, or even a bit silly, but taking the initiative and reaching out to rekindle relationships is almost always appreciated. The return on investment for the short amount of time it takes you to send some emails and texts, and hopefully make a few phone calls and lunch dates, is huge. You'll be left asking yourself, "Why didn't I do this sooner?"

3. Practice generosity—by finding little ways to help people.

You have two hands: one to help yourself and the second to help those around you.

It's one thing to take the initiative with people you already know, but what about all the people around you whom you barely know?

Be friendly and introduce yourself to someone nearby. When you're connecting with someone new, always start with generosity. Focus on how you can help the other person. Do you have information that could benefit them? Do you have a skill that could assist them through their current situation? Do you know someone they should meet?

One of the best investments you can make in yourself is to take a genuine interest in other people. The more you help others, the more they will want to help you. Love and kindness begets love and kindness. And so on and so forth.

4. Join an active community of like-minded people.

The best places to plant new seeds of friendship are at local, organized meetups on a particular topic that interests you. A meetup might be a professional association, a community focus group, a fitness class, a weekly group meditation hour, or any other gathering of people who share a common passion.

The easiest way to find a community to join is to make a list of your core passions and keywords that represent them. Think about everything you enjoy and every issue that has meaning to you. For example:

- Personal development
- Spirituality
- Blogging
- Software development
- Graphic design
- Acoustic guitar
- Meditation
- Yoga
- Cooking

Just let loose, open your mind, and do a brain dump onto a piece of paper. When you're finished, head to Meetup.com, type in your keywords, and see what you can find. Alternately, add the name of your city to your keywords and use them as a Google search query (for example: "cooking class Austin"). This will help you find local meetups, social groups, bloggers, businesses, and events related to these topics.

What if you can't find a meetup group that fits your needs? Start one. Of course, the disadvantage of being a founder and organizer is that it takes a little more time and energy. The upside, however, is everything else.

Finding the right group of people who share your passions and interests may require some dedicated research, but it's worth it. A shared passion is the most effective component in building positive, lasting relationships.

5. Reach out to leaders and mentors.

When we were in the process of mind-mapping ideas for launching our first book, *1,000+ Little Things Happy, Successful People Do Differently*, and researching ways to take our blog to the next level, we started reading and watching material from Derek Halpern, Ramit Sethi, and Lewis Howes, three down-to-earth guys who are masters in the online business space. We took inspiration from each of them and gradually implemented their ideas for our book launch.

Then we thought, "Why not email them?" So we did.

And they all replied.

Next thing you know, we're exchanging emails and tweets, and then when we were visiting New York City (where they all live), we got in touch and we all got together for a fun Sunday brunch.

The lesson here: Don't limit yourself. Take a look at the blogs you have bookmarked, the email lists you subscribe to, or even your bookshelf, for example, and ask yourself, "Which of these bloggers, authors, and entrepreneurs might I like to get to know?" And then reach out to them.

Bloggers, authors, and internet entrepreneurs in particular seem to be more easily accessible by email and social media than other public figures. Obviously, you may never meet or even get a personal response from some of the people you contact this way, but it's still fun to make an attempt, and you never know what will happen. You just might make a solid connection with someone who inspires you.

Nowadays we make it a point to email at least one person every month whom we would love to know more about, and whom we might normally consider out of reach. More than half of these people have replied back to us.

Next Steps for Building New, Healthy Relationships

If these points make sense to you, but you're still struggling with what seems to be unhealthy, unsupportive relationships in your life, then we have a suggestion for you: Make a list of the five people you spend the most time with and your top three personal/professional values and goals. Then compare the lists.

Are the people you spend the most time with congruent with your values and goals?

Are *you* and your daily rituals congruent with your values and goals?

If not, it's time to make some positive changes—it's time to get comfortable (and proficient) standing on your own two feet, reaching out to others with a helping hand, and meeting some brand-new, like-minded people who can bring positive energy into your life.

A few years ago, we actually moved from San Diego to Austin to live near Thanh and other inspiring, like-minded entrepreneurs in the personal-development niche because we knew we needed to be surrounded by the right people and energy while we were making some significant lifestyle and business changes. And let us assure you, we experienced incredible, productive breakthroughs because of it!

The bottom line is that you need to get your mindset and rituals in order, and spend more time in a positive environment with positive people.

How to Build Solid Relationships (with Enormously Successful People)

OVER THE YEARS, we have written a lot about our personal struggles. But a related topic we haven't addressed nearly as often is our professional struggles. We help our course students with various aspects of career and business strategy every day, and yet we rarely write about it publicly. But we get emails from blog readers all the time asking the same fundamental question:

How do I find successful mentors who will help me reach my professional and business goals?

First, a quick story about life and business . . .

Many moons ago, when we were young twentysomething entrepreneurs who were struggling to get our business off the ground (with little money and basically no connections), we realized that if we ever intended to achieve our dreams, we needed guidance and mentorship from some successful people who had already walked the path we were embarking on.

So we did the most naive thing anybody could think of: We wrote cold email inquiries to the (basically famous) A-listers of our industry—bloggers with millions of monthly readers, bestselling authors, social entrepreneurs and coaches with ridiculously successful businesses, and the list goes on. We let them know that we admired specific professional decisions they had made and certain character traits they had displayed publicly over the years, and that it would be a dream come true if we could learn directly from them, perhaps by volunteering our time to assist them with some of their active projects.

We should have known better, right?

These were some of the busiest people on planet Earth! Who were we to think that they would reply to a couple of twentysomething dreamers with no publicly recognizable skills whatsoever, beyond, perhaps, the ability to write a coherent email? And we subtly asked them to offer us their mentorship, and we suggested we would volunteer, when they obviously already had successful teams of people they trusted . . . We were *nuts*, weren't we?

Then an unimaginable thing happened. We received an email reply . . . and a second . . . and a third . . . and over the next few years we found ourselves learning from and being directly and indirectly mentored by an enormously successful group of people who were undoubtedly our biggest heroes at the time.

For quite a while, as we were in the thick of learning and growing, we never really stopped to question why everyone was being so nice to us. One day, several years later, five of these same mentors—who were now our friends—joined us for a face-to-face mastermind meeting that was part of a conference we were hosting. And one of them randomly joked that she had gotten to know us through a cold email inquiry we once sent her. The room went quiet for a moment. Then, at the same exact time, our other four mentors who were present in the room started snickering and nodding their heads in agreement that they, too, had met us through a simple, cold email inquiry.

The whole room broke out in sincere laughter.

"Do you know why I decided to meet with you both?" one of them asked.

We smiled and just looked at each other.

"Because after a couple decades of running my business, every single person who reached out to me with a cold inquiry wanted something from me. They wanted my money, they wanted me to give them a job . . . they wanted something for free. Your inquiry caught my attention because you two were the first ones who wanted to give me something, and actually showed a well-researched, genuine interest in learning more about the projects I was working on and excited about."

We looked around the room. The others were again nodding their heads in agreement.

Needless to say, we learned something important about life and business that day.

FRIENDSHIPS & EVERYDAY RELATIONSHIP QUESTIONS TO MAKE *YOU* THINK

Why do some good relationships go bad?

What would happen if you surrounded yourself with people who made you better?

What's one clear sign you might be hanging out with the wrong crowd?

What are your experiences with toxic friendships?

How can we better recognize toxic friendships?

What's one thing a true friend would never do?

In your experience, what helps create a happy, long-lasting friendship?

What do you want to thank your best friends for?

What would you like your best friends to thank you for?

Are *you* and your daily rituals congruent with your goals and values?

PART FIVE

. . . . .

Conflict & Drama

Walk Away or Change Perspectives

WHEN WE THINK about conflict and drama, what we're hoping for—likely what anyone hopes for—is to avoid them. And, of course, that's not always possible. More often than not, you're contending with other people's mood swings and drama, the things in their life that cause conflict for you. And a lot of the time, the drama is worthy—there are people who are experiencing pain, going through their own hardships, and you're going to have to deal with those issues. That can be a beautiful thing, because it gives you the opportunity to practice patience, to be more mindful of the hurting human being around you, to realize that hurt people hurt people.

So when you feel attacked, when you feel the drama and negativity coming your way, it gives you the opportunity to pause so that you can respond more effectively. It gives you the opportunity to be a bigger person right in the heat of the moment. That's the hard stuff. Saying this is easy. It seems simple, right? The steps are actually quite simple. And yet the practice of controlling your emotions, of giving yourself that five seconds, of taking a deep breath so that you can respond rather than react is a practice that must be exercised.

So how can we do that?

What are some methods that allow us to identify what works and what doesn't?

The biggest thing that helps us deal with conflict and drama is to be okay, to be well in our own mind.

Your own practice of self-care is probably your first line of defense in dealing with other people's conflict and drama. Let's use an example. If every day for weeks Angel has practiced what she needs personally—her quiet time in the morning, her time for meditation, her time to journal, her time to go to the float studio and decompress, her time to sort through and sit with her own thoughts—then when she comes into the household and, let's say, Marc's having a bad day and bringing some drama and conflict to the table, she's much better able to manage it. That's because she's done the things that she needs to do for herself. When you identify your own needs in this area, realizing that you need to fill your bucket first, then when your bucket is full, you can be a source of peace, mindfulness, and care for those around you who are experiencing conflict and drama.

From there, you can begin to realize and acknowledge that there is conflict and drama that is worth engaging with further, and there is conflict and drama that is not. If someone at work, who is not your immediate supervisor, is creating conflict and drama in the office by gossiping about people, or being rude and generally antagonistic, you can choose to stay away from it. There's no reason to have a conversation with that person or about that person, or even to partake in any bit of the conversation that they're having. If someone who's in your community is causing drama, has been rude to you, or is just being a jerk, walk away.

However, if it's your spouse, your child, your parent, your sibling, or someone you love whom you see on a regular basis, who matters to you, and they're bringing the conflict and drama, then that is a situation worth engaging in, right? We don't recommend engaging in the drama, but rather shifting from the drama to communication and being the bigger person. You can be a source of peace by not expecting the other person to change and by considering their perspective.

If someone is being a negative source in your life, naysaying your situation, and you're not feeling support from them, how can you try to see things from their point of view? Let's say you tell your dad about something you're working on and his response to you is negative, about how it's a bad idea and a waste of time. Remember, it's not personal. Many times people speak from the boundaries of their own limitations and understanding about life.

So ask yourself: Has your dad walked the same path before you? Has he been where you're going to be? If the answer is yes, then there's no need to take his negativity to heart, but it may be worth opening your ears and eyes to what he's trying to teach you. But if the answer is no, then it's almost certain that because he himself has never done it, he's likely fearful for you. He may not be communicating in the most effective way, but he loves you and could be trying to tell you, "Hey, listen— this isn't a risk I would take, and I don't want my daughter or son taking that risk either."

Think about that example and how you can extrapolate it into other circumstances, realizing that a lot of times the conflict or drama coming from someone you love has nothing to do with you. We have to give ourselves a five-second pause to truly listen to the other human being and see things from their perspective. We won't always change what the other person has to say, but we can change how we interpret it in a way that won't affect us as greatly.

8 Things to Remember When Your Relationship Gets Rough

YOU NEVER KNOW when life is about to teach you a new lesson. You simply can't plan for it. Some lessons seem to sneak up on you when you least expect them. This is especially true when it comes to relationships. There have been times in our personal and professional relationships when we wish a lesson had come a bit earlier, to save us from heartache and the wasted time and energy of learning things the hard way.

That being said, we are grateful for every lesson our relationships have taught us over the years because we are now better equipped to deal with rough patches when they arise. And that's exactly what we want to cover with you here—eight things we've learned to keep in mind when a relationship gets rough. These aren't solutions to specific problems, but rather simple reminders that will help you look at many common relationship problems more objectively.

1. Every one of us is struggling in some way.

It's impossible to know exactly how another person is feeling or what kind of emotional battles they're fighting. Sometimes the widest smiles hide the thinnest strands of self-confidence and hope. Sometimes the rich have everything but happiness. Realize this as you interact with others, long before you pass judgment. Every smile or sign of strength hides an inner struggle every bit as complex and extraordinary as your own.

It's a sage fact of life, really, that every one of us encompasses a profound and unique set of secrets and mysteries that are absolutely undetectable to everyone else, including those closest to us.

2. Some people will put you down no matter what you do.

Yes, there will be those who are critical of you regardless of what you do or how well you do it. If you say you want to be a dancer, they will discredit your rhythm. If you say you want to build a new business, they will give you a dozen reasons why it might not work. They somehow assume you don't have what it takes, but they are dead wrong.

Do not engage deeply in a relationship that is holding you back day in and day out.

It's a lot easier to be negative than positive—a lot easier to be critical than correct. When you're embarking on a new venture, instead of listening to the few critics who will try to discredit you, spend time talking to one of the millions of people in this world who are willing to support your efforts and acknowledge your potential.

3. Resentment hurts only its holder.

Holding a resentful grudge is like drinking toxic venom and waiting for the other person to grow ill. It's an exercise in futility. And just as venom is toxic to the human body, so is resentment to the human spirit—even one tiny bit is bad for you

Don't magnify life's difficulties by filling your mind with resentment. Instead, ease your burdens by choosing to let them go. If you feel resentment starting to take hold, stop to consider the fact that there's nothing to be gained by bringing yourself down over what has already happened.

Let today be the day you stop letting the ghosts of yesterday haunt you. Let today be the day you stop poisoning yourself with needless hatred. Forget about getting even with someone who has hurt you, and instead get even with those who have helped.

4. Forgiveness is the only path to peace of mind.

When someone has hurt you, it's hard to be peaceful. But you do it anyway because you know peace is the only battle worth waging. Peace is beautiful; it is the manifestation of your love and the best resolution for a brighter future.

Being peaceful is hard sometimes—much harder than being angry and vengeful. It requires you to stay calm and let go of the pain. It requires you to forgive and move on. Of course, you don't do these things just for the person who has hurt you, but for your own well-being.

5. True love is real and worth working for.

Whether it's a friendship or an intimate relationship, when someone loves you, you know it. When they look your way, the world looks better. When they say your name, the world sounds better. When they touch your skin, the world feels better. You know your soul is safe in their care.

But even more so than any physical interaction, there's a silent connection between you that you can feel in your veins. You can sit in front of them for hours, without saying a word or moving a muscle, and yet still feel them with your heart. It's almost like they've always been a part of you—like a long lost fragment of your essence has found its way home.

It's important to note, though, that you learn about this kind of love slowly as a relationship grows. It's not something you realize all at once. It's about how two people treat each other, respect each other, and work together over a prolonged period, through good times and bad.

6. It is our imperfections that ultimately attract us to each other.

If you're still searching for the perfect partner or friend, stop. There's no such thing. There are only different flavors of imperfect ones. In fact, you are just as imperfect as the partner or friend you seek. You simply need to find someone whose imperfections complement your own.

This process doesn't happen overnight.

It takes a lot of living to grow into the realization of your own imperfections. It takes lots of life experience before you bump into your deepest inner demons, your greatest flaws, and all the idiosyncrasies that make you, *you*. And it's only after you meet these imperfect parts of yourself that you know who you are looking for—someone whose scars and flaws fit your own; someone who is imperfect in the perfect way for you.

7. We all bring positivity and negativity into our relationships.

Be careful not to continuously doubt the positives of your partner (or friend) and then ignore your own negative behavior. You likely do this more often than you think. For instance, you will say to your partner dozens of times, "Do you really love me? Are you sure?" And ask similar questions that doubt the existence of their love. But you will rarely ask, "Does this upset you? Are you sure?" And similar questions that have the potential to resolve conflict before it starts.

This imbalance creates tension on both sides of the equation. The positive things become more burdensome, while the negatives fester in the background, unresolved. Bottom line: Have faith in the positives as you work on turning the negatives around, or simply accepting them.

8. Spending time alone is necessary.

Relationships with others are important, but you need alone time sometimes, because when you're in solitude, you're free from obligations and external pressures. You're free to be *you* without being fancy and putting on a show. You're able to hear your own thoughts and follow through with them, sincerely.

Go ahead and find a quiet place. Stretch your boundaries. Explore places you've never been. Go so far away from what you know that you stop being afraid of the unfamiliar.

Cherish your time alone. Take long walks and drives by yourself. Watch sunsets and sunrises silently in peace. Teach yourself something new. Read books. Write poetry. Sing along to your favorite songs. Check your instincts and follow them on your own time, without third-party influence. Decide if fitting in 24/7 is more important than discovering who you truly are and what you're here to do. Once you've got a handle on this, relationships with others get a lot easier.

Afterthoughts

All relationships, including the one you have with yourself, require patience and work. No meaningful relationship will work flawlessly all the time. Being too black and white about the expectations of what should or shouldn't happen in a relationship always spells trouble. No matter what, there will be difficulties, but you can still focus on the good. Instead of constantly looking for signs of what's not working in your relationships, what you need to do is look for signs of what is. Because, as you know, what we focus on grows.

7 Things to Remember When You Feel Cheated On

SOMETIMES WE FEEL cheated on by others.

Sometimes we feel cheated on by our circumstances.

Sometimes we feel cheated on by life itself.

In any case, we are faced with the reality that things aren't always what they seem—we don't always get what we expect. And we begin to learn that our expectations are like fine pottery—the harder we hold on to them, the more likely they are to crack wide open.

So what can we do?

Embrace reality, and make the best of it.

The truth is, we were promised trials and tribulations right from the beginning. They were always part of the program. Growing up, we were told, "What doesn't kill us makes us stronger." And we have learned to accept it. The relationships, jobs, and projects that didn't work out led us closer to the ones that did. The things we've lost too soon opened our minds to understandings and opportunities we never fathomed beforehand. So while we've rarely gotten exactly what we wanted, we've often received more than we bargained for.

Of course, in the heat of the moment, when disappointing things are happening to *you*, not to others, and the outcomes you're dealing with are *real*, not imagined, embracing reality and making the best of it is not easy.

You feel cheated on.

You feel victimized.

You feel crushed.

Which is why, first and foremost, it's important to . . .

Learn to Be Mindful of Your Expectations

Imagine you had a ripe, juicy apple sitting on a table in front of you. You pick it up eagerly, take a nibble, and begin to taste it.

You already know how an apple should taste, and so when this one is a bit more tart than you expected, you make a face, feel a sense of disappointment, and swallow it, feeling cheated out of a good experience.

Or perhaps the apple tastes *exactly* as you expected—nothing special at all. So you swallow without even pausing to enjoy its flavor, and you move on with your day.

In the first scenario, the apple let you down because it didn't meet your expectations. In the second, it was too plain and unexciting because it met your expectations to a T.

Do you see the irony here?

It's either not good or not good enough.

This is how many of us live our lives . . . unhappily.

It's why many of us feel cheated on, victimized, and crushed far too often.

Now imagine you try this instead: Eliminate your expectations of how the apple "should" taste. You don't know, and you don't pretend to know, because you haven't tried it yet. Instead you're genuinely curious, impartial, and open to a variety of flavors.

You taste it, and you truly pay attention. You notice the juiciness, the grainy texture of the skin, the simultaneously sweet, tangy, and tart flavors swirling around your tongue, and all the other complex sensations that arise in your awareness as you chew. You didn't know how it would taste, but now you realize it's different from the rest, and it's remarkable in its own way. It's a totally new experience—a worthwhile experience—because you've never tasted *this* apple before.

Mindfulness practitioners often refer to this as "beginner's mind," but really it's just the outcome of a mindset free of needless and stressful expectations.

The apple, of course, can be substituted for anything in your life: any event, any circumstance, any relationship, any person, any thought at all that enters your mind, anytime and anyplace. If you approach any of these with expectations of "how it should be," they will surely disappoint you in some way . . . or be too plain and unexciting to remember.

And you'll just move on to the next disappointment or unexciting experience, and the next, and the next, and so on and so forth, until you've lived your entire life stuck in an endless cycle of things you barely like or barely even notice . . . until you kinda feel cheated on by everything and everyone you've ever known.

But if you approach each event, circumstance, relationship, etc., without expectations—and just see that moment at face value—then you will truly see it. You will truly experience it like you've never experienced anything before, because you haven't. And you will be able to mindfully respond to whatever happens next.

But (and There's Always a "But") . . .

Now that we've cleared the air a bit and established some healthy breathing room, let's get real about something else:

At some point, even when you've done your part to be mindful of your expectations, someone you trust or respect will deliberately hurt you. They will cheat on you in some way by placing their own self-centered agenda ahead of your feelings. And they will do it remorselessly, without an apology.

When you are faced with this reality, and you're struggling to cope, let us prompt you with some essential reminders that we often review with our course students who are struggling with similar circumstances:

1. The person who cheated on you is likely broken in more ways than you realize. When people cheat in any arena, they diminish themselves—they directly threaten their own self-esteem and their relationships with others by undermining the trust they have in their ability to succeed and in their ability to be true. In many ways, they are deeply broken. This, however, does *not* excuse their behavior.

2. The truth hurts, but it's much healthier than holding on to the lies you once believed. The really scary thing about undiscovered lies is that they have a greater capacity to diminish us in the long run than exposed lies. Undiscovered lies erode our strength, our self-esteem, our very foundation to the bitter end. Keep this in mind. The truth heals, even if it hurts at first.

3. Arguing with someone who has intentionally hurt you only enflames the pain. Truth be told, you are often most powerful and influential in an argument regarding betrayal when you are silent. The perpetrator never expects silence. They expect yelling, drama, defensiveness, offensiveness, and lots of back-and-forth. They expect to leap into the ring and fight. They are ready to defend themselves with sly remarks cocked and loaded. But your mindful silence? That can really disarm them. That can really give you the space you need to move forward, one way or another, with or without them.

4. It's always best to wish people well, even if they don't deserve it. If you spend your time and energy hoping someone will suffer the consequences for breaking your heart, then you're allowing them to hurt you a second time in your mind.

5. Healing gets easier when you learn to accept an apology you never received. Forgiveness is crucial for your healing. The key is to be mindful and grateful, despite what happened. It's taking a step back and saying, "Thank you for the lesson." When you forgive someone, you are making a promise not to hold the unchangeable past against your present self. It has nothing to do with freeing the perpetrator of his or her crime and everything to do with freeing yourself of the burden of being an eternal victim.

6. The person who hurt you doesn't speak for the rest of us. Every one of us suffers from at least one heart-wrenching betrayal in our lifetime. In a backward way, it's what unites us. When it happens to you, the key is not to let one person's despicable actions destroy your trust in others. Don't let them take that from you.

7. A wonderful, life-changing gift may not be wrapped as you expect. When you don't get what you want, sometimes it's necessary preparation, and other times it's necessary protection. But the time is never wasted. It's a step on your journey. Someday you're going to look back on this time in your life as an important time of grieving and growing. You will see that you were in mourning and your heart was breaking, but your life was changing for the greater good.

7 Things to Remember When You're Scared to Speak Up

IN THE EARLY 1990s, twelve-year-old Severn Cullis-Suzuki was passionately obsessed with real-world issues like poverty, ocean pollution, and global warming. She was just a child, but she also understood that the decisions adults made concerning these issues would impact her life and the lives of all children for generations to come. And she believed she and other children should have a voice and be present during critical global meetings on these issues.

Severn boldly set her sights on attending the next United Nations conference. At the time, in over fifty years, no child had ever attended a UN conference—a formal meeting where ambassadors from nearly every developed country come together to openly discuss the future health of the world. But Severn believed it was time to change this—it was time for children to have a voice too. So not only was she determined to attend, but she resolved to make sure her voice was heard loud and clear too.

Severn applied to attend the UN Conference on Environment and Development through the environmental nonprofit she and her friends founded when they were all just nine years old. And when her application was accepted—not because of her age but because she had helped build a relevant nonprofit—she knew it was just the beginning.

When Severn arrived at the UN conference, she hit the ground running with one goal in mind: to find an opportunity to publicly convey her message about the importance of children being a part of the UN's global conversation. Quickly, she learned that one of the scheduled speakers was unable to attend the conference. So she volunteered to replace that speaker. And although there was some initial reluctance, her offer was ultimately accepted.

A few days later, she stood on stage, utterly nervous, looked out over a room filled with ambassadors from around the world, and began speaking in a clear, steady voice. She may have been just twelve-years-old, and she may have felt out of her element, but her air of authority and passion were unmistakable: "I'm only a child, and I don't have all the solutions. But I want you to realize, neither do you."

When Severn wrapped up her speech and exited the stage, the ambassadors gave her a standing ovation. But more importantly, they heard her, and they took action. At the next UN Conference on Environment and Development children were invited to attend and participate. And it all happened because one twelve-year-old girl had the courage and tenacity to stand up for her right to be heard.

In a nutshell, that's the power of good communication!

And although Severn's story is just one interesting example of how good communication can be leveraged, let it inspire you to think about all the other incredible possibilities that can bloom when someone, of any age or stature, stands up and speaks intelligently from their heart.

IF YOU HAVE something meaningful to say, but you're scared to speak up, remember . . .

1. Not feeling ready to speak up could be a sign that you actually are ready. The more you live and learn—the more seasoned and educated you become—the more you will come to realize just how little you actually know in the grand scheme of things. Every human being deals with this phenomenon to a certain extent. Research suggests that the so-called impostor syndrome that takes place when we suddenly don't feel "good enough" or "ready yet" gets more intense as we grow wiser. In addition, the more experienced or knowledgeable we become, the more likely we are to compare ourselves with, or even rub shoulders with, ever more interesting, talented, and wise people, leaving us feeling even more inadequate by comparison. So, in a backward way, if you're concerned that you don't measure up—that you're not ready yet—it could very well be a sign that you actually do measure up just fine and that now is the time to speak up.

2. Most social conflicts between good people start with bad communication, or no communication. Too often we try to read each other's minds, to no avail, and then we sit back and wonder why we're all on different pages. Take this to heart. Say what you mean and mean what you say. Give the people in your life the information they need, rather than expecting them to know the unknowable. Speak clearly and honestly, and then listen sincerely.

3. The only way to find support is to admit how you feel in the first place. For example, sometimes we feel as though the world is crashing down around us, as if the pain we are experiencing is unique to us in the moment. This, of course, is far from the truth. We are all in this to-gether. The very demons that torment each of us torment all of us. It is our challenges and troubles that connect us at the deepest level.

4. The right words can be incredibly healing. When you grow older and you look back on your life, you will inevitably forget a lot of the stuff that seemed so important when you were young. You probably won't remember what your high school or college GPA was. You will look up your old classmates online and wonder why you ever had a crush on that guy or girl. And you will have the toughest time remembering why you let certain people from your past get the best of you. But you will never forget the people who were genuinely kind—those who helped when you were hurt, and who loved you even when you felt unlovable. Be that person to others when you can. Your voice can heal. Sometimes you will say something really small and simple, but it will fit right into an empty space in someone's heart.

5. Silence can be self-abuse. You have to admit that, to a certain extent, you have spent too much of your life trying to silence yourself. Trying to become quieter. Smaller. Less sensitive. Less needy. Less *you*. Because you didn't want to be too much for people. You wanted to make a good impression on them. You wanted to fit in. You wanted everyone to like you. So for much of your life, you've sacrificed a part of yourself—your need to be heard—for the sake of not stepping on anyone's toes. And for much of your life, you've abused yourself with your own silence. But you're tired of living this way, right? When you give yourself permission to openly communicate what matters to you, peace will develop within you despite the possible rejection or disapproval you may face. Putting a voice to your heart and soul helps you to let go and grow.

6. Honest communication can disarm people's difficult tendencies. We all have difficult people in our lives, but not all of them are difficult on purpose. Sometimes people who care about you—people who have decent intentions—are incredibly hard to deal with simply because they're struggling with their own issues. Such people need your support, but you must also be honest with them. Not confronting someone's difficult behavior can become the principal reason for being sucked into their drama. Challenging their behavior upfront, on the other hand, will sometimes get them to realize the negative impact of their actions. For instance, you might say, "I've noticed you seem angry. Is something upsetting you?" Or "Your attitude is upsetting me right now. Is this what you want?" Direct statements like these can be disarming if someone is subconsciously stuck in a rut, and these statements can also open doors of opportunity for you to help them if they're genuinely facing a serious problem. And even if they deny their behavior, at least you've made them aware that their attitude has become a known issue to someone else.

7. Your voice can bring people together. We know this is true because, over the past decade, we have coached hundreds of people of different ethnic backgrounds, from different cities and countries, who live at various socioeconomic levels, and every single one of these people basically wants what we want. We *all* want validation, love, happiness, fulfillment, financial stability, and hopes for a better future. The unique ways we pursue these "wants" is where things branch off, but the fundamentals are the same. So whenever possible, find the courage to use your voice to help those around you see the world through commonalities of the human heart and soul—remind them that we're all in this together. This is how humanity as a whole gradually evolves and grows stronger. The language of the heart and soul—of togetherness—is mankind's common language. When we change the way we communicate with each other, we change society for the better.

Speaking Up Is Not About Engaging in Drama

With all the aforementioned said, keep in mind that constantly talking and challenging others isn't communicating. It's just drama. You are as powerful as the meaningful ideas you share with others, and you are as wise as the selective silence you leave behind. Think of Severn Suzuki again. She didn't just speak—she had something decisive and meaningful to say.

So do your best to be wise with your words. There is a time to speak up and a time to remain quiet. Knowledge is knowing what to say. Wisdom is knowing whether or not to say it.

Of course, the "wisdom" of striking the right balance will take practice, and that's okay. Just speak from your heart and soul—with kindness and the intention to add value—and you will gradually learn not to waste words on moments that deserve your silence.

Afterthoughts

In closing, we'd like to lighten the mood and leave you with a joke on communication recently told by Ellen DeGeneres:

"Not only have we given up on writing letters to each other, we barely even talk to each other these days. People have become so accustomed to texting that they're actually startled when the phone rings. It's like we suddenly all have Batphones. If it rings, there must be danger.

"Now we answer, 'What happened? Is someone tied up in the old sawmill?'

"'No, it's Becky. I just called to say hi.'

"'Well, you scared me half to death. You can't just pick up the phone and try to talk to me like that. Don't the tips of your fingers work?'"

At the very least, we hope this article inspires you to speak up by picking up the phone today, just to say something meaningful to someone you care about.

9 Mindful Ways to Remain Calm When Others Are Angry

AS HUMAN BEINGS, we all have an idea in our heads about how things are supposed to be, and sadly this is what often messes our relationships up the most. We all get frustrated when things don't play out the way we expect them to, and people don't behave like they're "supposed" to. We expect our spouses and children to act a certain way, our friends to be kind and agreeable, strangers to be less difficult, and so on and so forth.

And when reality hits us, and everyone seems to be doing the opposite of what we want them to do, we overreact—anger, frustration, stress, arguments, tears, etc.

So what can we do about this?

Breathe . . .

You can't control how other people behave. You can't control everything that happens to you. What you can control is how you respond to it all. In your response is your power.

When you feel like your lid is about to blow, take a long, deep breath. Deep breathing releases tension, calms down our fight-or-flight reactions, and allows us to quiet our anxious nerves so that we choose more considerate and constructive responses, no matter the situation.

So, for example, do your best to inhale and exhale the next time another driver cuts you off in traffic. As mentioned in the Introduction, in a recent poll we hosted with 1,200 new course students, overreacting while fighting traffic was the most commonly cited reason for overreacting on a daily basis. Just imagine if all the drivers on the road took deep breaths before making nasty hand gestures or screaming obscenities at others.

There's no doubt that it can drive us crazy when we don't get what we expect from people, especially when they are being rude and difficult. But trying to change the unchangeable, wanting others to be exactly the way we want them to be, just doesn't work. The alternative, though, is unthinkable to most of us: to breathe, to let go, to lead by example, and to accept people even when they irritate us.

Here's the way of being that we cultivate and advocate:

- Breathe deeply and often.
- Remind ourselves that we can't control other people.
- Remind ourselves that other people can handle their lives however they choose.
- Don't take their behavior personally.
- See the good in them.
- Let go of the ideals and expectations we have about others that cause unnecessary frustration, arguments, and bouts of anger.
- Remember that when others are being difficult, they are often going through a difficult time we know nothing about. And give them empathy, love, and space.

Being this way takes practice, but it's worth it. It makes us less frustrated, it helps us to be more mindful, it improves our relationships, it lowers our stress, and it allows us to make the world a slightly more peaceful place to be. We hope you will join us.

Smart Ways to Remain Calm

If you're ready to feel more peace and less inner angst, here are some ways we've learned to remain calm and centered, even when those around us can't seem to contain themselves. These principles reinforce the previous bullet points, and when you consistently practice these principles, the world within you and around you becomes a lot easier to cope with.

Let's practice, together . . .

1. Get comfortable with pausing.

Don't imagine the worst when you encounter a little drama. When someone is acting irrationally, don't join them by rushing to make a negative judgment call. Instead, pause. Take a deep breath . . .

Sometimes good people behave poorly under stress. Don't you? When you pause, it gives you space to collect your thoughts and it also allows the other person the space to take a deep breath with you. In most cases, that extra time and space is all we need.

2. Respect people's differences.

Learn to respect the opinions of others. Just because someone does it differently doesn't make it wrong. There are many roads to what's right in this world. Everyone is entitled to their own opinion.

So choose your battles wisely. And just agree to disagree sometimes.

It is absolutely possible to connect with, and even appreciate the company of, someone you don't completely agree with. When you make a commitment to remain neutral on topics that don't matter that much, or speak respectfully about your disagreements, both parties can remain calm and move forward, pleasantly.

3. Be compassionate.

In the busyness of today's world, people tend to be worried, fearful, hurting, and distracted about everything. The word "compassion" means "to suffer with." When you can put yourself in the other person's shoes, you give them the space to regroup, without putting any extra pressure on them.

Remember, we never know what's really going on in someone's life. When you interact with others in stressful environments, set an intention to be supportive by leaving the expectations, judgments, and demands at the door.

4. Extend generosity and grace.

Everyone gets upset and loses their temper sometimes. Remind yourself that we are all more alike than we are different. When you catch yourself passing judgment, add "just like me sometimes" to the end of a sentence. For example:

- That person is grouchy, just like me sometimes.
- He is so darn impatient, just like me sometimes.
- She is being rude, just like me sometimes.

Choose to let things *go*. Let others off the hook. Take the high road today.

5. Don't take people's behavior personally.

We've said it before and we'll say it again, if you take everything personally, you will be offended for the rest of your life. And there's no reason for it. You may not be able control all the things people say and do to you, but you can decide not to be reduced by them. Make that decision for yourself today.

Let it go! Seriously, there is a huge amount of freedom that comes when you detach yourself from other people's beliefs and behaviors. The way people treat you is their problem; how you react is yours.

Everyone behaves the way they behave based on how they feel inside. Some people never learn how to effectively cope with their stressful emotions. When someone is acting obnoxious, it's vital that you remain calm, no matter what. Don't allow other people to knock you off your center.

Do what it takes to remain calm and address the situation from the inside out. That's where your greatest power lies.

6. Talk less and learn to appreciate silence.

Don't fall into an unnecessary argument just because you feel uncomfortable in silence. Don't say things you'll regret five minutes later just to fill your eardrums with noise. Anger and frustration begin internally. You have the capacity to choose your response to momentary discomfort. Inhale. Exhale. A moment of silence in a moment of anger can save you from a hundred moments of regret.

7. Create a morning ritual that starts your day off right.

Don't rush into your day by checking your phone or email. Don't put yourself in a stressful state of mind that makes you incapable of dealing positively with other people's negativity. Create time and space for a morning ritual that's focused and peaceful.

Here's part of Angel's morning ritual: She takes ten deep breaths before getting out of bed, stands up and stretches, and then does ten minutes of meditation.

We challenge you to try this—it has been life-changing for

Angel—but start small, with just three deep breaths and three minutes of meditation a day. Do this for thirty days. After thirty days, if this daily ritual becomes easy, add another two breaths and another two minutes to your ritual. When you begin a day mindfully, you lay the foundation for your day to be calm and centered, regardless of what's going on around you.

8. Cope using healthy choices and alternatives.

When we face stressful situations, we often calm or soothe ourselves with unhealthy choices—drinking alcohol, eating sugary snacks, smoking, etc. It's easy to respond to anger with anger and unhealthy distractions.

Notice how you cope with stress. Replace bad coping habits with healthy coping habits. Take a walk in a green space. Make a cup of tea and sit quietly with your thoughts. Listen to some pleasant music. Write in your journal. Talk it out with a close friend. Healthy coping habits make happy people.

9. Remind yourself of what's right, and create more of it in the world.

Keeping the positive in mind helps you move beyond the negativity around you.

At the end of the day, reflect on your small daily wins and all the little things that are going well. Count three small events on your fingers that happened during the day that you're undoubtedly grateful for. For example:

- My family and I made it home safely from work and school today.
- My spouse and I shared a laugh.
- We have everything we need to feel safe and cared for.

And pay it forward when you get a chance. Let your positivity empower you to think kindly of others, speak kindly to others, and do kind things for others. Kindness always makes a difference. Create the outcomes others might be grateful for at the end of their day. Be a bigger part of what's right in this world.

The most fundamental aggression to ourselves and others—the most fundamental harm we can do to human nature as a whole—is to remain ignorant by not having the awareness and the courage to look at ourselves and others honestly and gently.

Should I Forgive Him? Should I Forgive Her? Here's What You Should Ask Yourself First

Never Forgive Him

A friend showed up at our front door before work at 7:00 a.m. one morning with the most troubled, despondent expression on her face (which is not typical of her disposition). Angel invited her in and poured her a cup of coffee so they could talk.

"Last night my husband told me something about his college years that he never told me before," she said in a shaky voice. "And I completely disagree with his actions. It's horrible, really . . . and I just can't stop thinking about it! I don't know if I will ever be able to forgive him."

"Well, before you tell me anything else, let me ask you this: Why do you think your husband confided in you? I mean, why do you think he told you now?"

"I don't know," she replied. "I guess he finally trusted me enough to tell me."

"Did he commit a crime?"

"No."

"Was anyone physically or emotionally hurt by his actions?"

"No, not really."

"So, how do you feel about him right now? Do you still love him?"

"Of course I do," she replied.

"And whatever he did back in college, do you think he learned his lesson? Or do you think he would do it again?"

"Oh, I'm fairly certain he learned a big lesson," she replied. "He actually teared up about it when he told me—he said he's still ashamed of himself."

"Okay, so let me see if I fully understand the situation then . . . Last night your husband finally felt that he trusted you enough to tell you about a dark secret from his college years. And although somewhat unsettling, he didn't hurt anyone, and you think he learned his lesson, which means he grew emotionally from the experience. And to top it off, you're still completely in love with him. So, what exactly can you never forgive him for?"

She sat in silence for a few seconds, made a crooked half smile, and then shook her head. Then she started laughing. And so did Angel.

More About Us, Less About Them

Sometimes the problems we have with others—our spouse, parents, siblings, and so on—don't really have much to do with them at all, because these problems are actually about us.

And that's okay. It simply means these little predicaments will be easier to solve. We are, after all, in charge of our own decisions. We get to decide whether we want to keep our head cluttered with events from the past, or whether instead we open our minds to the positive realities unfolding in front of us.

All we need is the willingness to look at things a little differently—letting go of "what happened" and "what should never have been," and instead focusing our energy on "what is" and "what could be possible."

Because, as our friend discovered that morning, sometimes the only problem standing in our way is the one we created in our head.

Does Anything Really Need to Be Forgiven Here?

That's a question we challenge you to ask yourself first, whenever you feel like our friend felt when she arrived at our doorstep. It's a simple question that can provide a necessary dose of perspective when your emotions are surging. And it's a practice we often discuss with our course students and live-event attendees when forgiveness is at stake in their personal relationships.

The bottom line is that letting go of the need to process every little misstep and mistake a person makes can be mentally and emotionally freeing for everyone involved. Make that decision, and feel the freedom.

Truly, there is an obvious shift in our hearts and minds that happens when we go from feeling hurt and upset to feeling peaceful and loving, but it's not necessarily forgiveness that's taking place—it's just the realization that there was nothing to forgive in the first place. Because mistakes are the growing pains of wisdom, and sometimes they just need to be accepted with no strings attached.

To help you wrap your head around this concept, try to look at your situation from a distance. Imagine a more seasoned, wiser, and more compassionate version of yourself sitting at the mountaintop of life, looking down and watching as the younger-minded, present version of you stumbles your way through life.

You see yourself holding on to false beliefs and making obvious errors of judgment as you maneuver through life's many obstacles. You watch the children of the world growing up in challenging times that test their sense of self-confidence, yet they push forward bravely. You see the coming generation radiating with passion and love as they fail forward, learning through their mistakes.

And you have to wonder: Would this wiser version of yourself conclude that almost everyone in their own unique way was doing their best, or at least trying to? And if everyone is trying to do their best, what really needs to be forgiven? Not being perfect?

Obviously, there is *not* a one-size-fits-all answer to anything in life, and forgiveness is no exception. Some situations are far more complicated than others. But in any case, let's do our best to challenge our minds with a necessary dose of perspective whenever our emotions are surging. Let's learn from our mistakes, and let others learn from theirs. Let's embrace our imperfections, and let others embrace theirs ...

And let's begin again, together, with a little more acceptance, compassion, and peace of mind.

Ultimately, forgiveness is recognizing the reality that what has happened has already happened, and that there's no point in allowing it to dominate the rest of your life. Forgiveness refreshingly cleans the slate and enables you to step forward. Here are two unique ways to make this step possible:

1. Be the watcher of your thoughts and emotions.

In his bestselling book *The Power of Now*, Eckhart Tolle tells us to be the watcher of our thoughts. What he suggests is that instead of trying to change our thoughts—via gratitude or deliberate forgiveness, for example—we need to simply notice our thoughts without getting caught up in them.

You are ultimately the sole creator of your own feelings. When negative thoughts arise based on past experiences or future worries, as they sometimes will, realize that these are simply issues your mind (not you) is working through. Pause, be present, and pay close attention. Think about these thoughts and emotions consciously, almost as if you were a bystander looking in. Separate yourself from your mind's thinking.

Perhaps after you study your thoughts and emotions you will think to yourself, "Wow, am I really still working through that?" And guess what? Over time, your negative feelings and emotions will lessen and genuine awareness, love, and acceptance will grow in their place. You will begin to realize that your mind is just an instrument, and you are in control of your mind, not the other way around.

By not judging your thoughts or blaming them on anyone else, and merely watching them, there will be a big shift within you—your sense of self-worth.

It's not like you won't get upset anymore or never feel anxious, but knowing that your thoughts and emotions are just fleeting feelings that are independent of *you* will help ease your tension and increase your positive presence, allowing you to forgive and let go.

2. Love.

Feeling sorry for yourself and sabotaging the present moment with resentful thoughts of the past won't make anything better. Hurting someone else will never ease your own inner angst.

If you're disappointed with yourself or frustrated with someone else, the answer is not to take it out on the world around you. Retribution, whether it's focused on yourself or others, brings zero value into your life.

The way beyond the pain from the past is not with vengeance, mockery, or bullying, but with present love.

Forgive the past, forgive yourself, forgive others, and love the present moment for what it's worth. There are plenty of beautiful things to love right now; you just have to want to see them. Loving is never easy, especially when times are tough, yet it is easily the most powerful and positively enduring action possible.

If you're feeling pain, don't take an action that creates even more pain. Don't try to cover darkness with darkness. Find the light. Act out of love. Do something that will enable you to move forward toward a more fulfilling reality. There is always something good you can do. There is always love to give. Fill your heart with it and act in everyone's best interest, especially your own.

Leverage your love to forgive yourself for the bad decisions you made, for the times you lacked understanding, for the choices that hurt others and yourself. Forgive yourself for being young and reckless. These are all vital lessons. And what matters most right now is your willingness to grow from them.

20 Powerful Mantras to Stop the Drama in Your Life

WHY DO WE get so easily stressed out and sucked into drama?

It's because the world isn't the predictable, orderly, blissful place we'd like it to be. We want things to be easy, comfortable, and well ordered. Unfortunately, work is hectic, relationships are challenging, people demand our time, we aren't as prepared as we'd like to be, our family frustrates us, and there's just too much to do and learn and process in our minds.

So we get stressed out, and drama ensues.

But the problem isn't the world, or other people's thoughts and behavior—these aspects of life will always be uncontrollable and a bit of a mess.

The problem is that we're holding on too tightly to ideals that don't match reality. We have subconsciously set up expectations in our minds of what we want other people to be, what we want ourselves to be, and what our work and relationships and life "should" be like.

Our attachment to our ideals stirs anxiety in our minds and stress in our lives.

Our resistance to accept things as they are fuels our drama.

And we don't want to be a part of this drama—at least that's what we tell ourselves—so we blame others for it . . . which in turn creates even more of it.

But there's good news! We can let go of drama and find peace with reality.

The Peace and Joy of No Drama

We're going to suggest a simple practice for whenever you feel stress, frustration, worry, and all the other detrimental mindsets that bring drama into your life.

Ready?

Focus carefully on what you're feeling. Don't numb it with distractions, but instead bring it further into your awareness.

Turn to it and welcome it. Smile, and give your full, thoughtful attention to what you feel.

Notice the feeling in your body. Where is the feeling situated, and what unique qualities does it have?

Notice the tension in your body, and also in your mind, that arises from this feeling.

Try relaxing the tense parts of your body. Then relax the tense parts of your mind. Do so by focusing on your breath: Close your eyes, breathe in, breathe out, again and again, until you feel more relaxed.

In this more relaxed state, find some quiet space within yourself. And in this space . . .

- Allow yourself to rediscover the fundamental goodness within you that's present in every moment.
- Allow yourself to rediscover the fundamental goodness of this very moment that's always available to you whenever you're willing to focus on it.

Take a moment and just sit with the inner peace these two simple rediscoveries bring.

This is the practice of letting go of drama, and simply accepting this moment as it is, and yourself as you are.

You can do this anytime, wherever you are. You can practice focusing on the goodness in others as well. See the goodness in your challenges and relationships and work and so forth. You can stop the drama and rediscover the peace and joy and love that are always close by.

Mantras to Help Stop the Drama

Since, like you, we're only human, we still engage in drama when we're in the heat of the moment sometimes. So we've implemented a simple strategy to support the practice we've outlined above. In a nutshell, we proactively remind ourselves *not* to create or engage in drama. Anytime we catch ourselves doing so, we pause and read the following mantras to ourselves (we keep them on our iPhones). Then we take some fresh deep breaths and begin our practice . . .

1. Needless drama doesn't just walk into your life out of nowhere—you either create it, invite it, or associate with those who bring it.

2. Do your best not to judge other people, for you do not know their pain or sorrow. If you cannot speak a kind word, say nothing at all. And if *they* cannot speak a kind word, say nothing at all.

3. Most people make themselves unhappy simply by finding it impossible to accept life just as it is presenting itself right now. Be mindful. Sometimes you just need to slow down, stay calm, and let things happen.

4. When you are no longer able to change a situation, you are challenged to change yourself. And that changes everything.

5. Don't bother worrying about whether there will be problems. There will be plenty of them, and you'll work your way through every one of them.

6. Worrying is a misuse of your incredible creative energy. Instead of imagining the worst, imagine the best and how you can bring it about.

7. When you focus your heart and mind upon a purpose, and commit yourself to fulfill that purpose through small daily steps, positive energy floods into your life.

8. It's okay to make mistakes. That's how you get wiser. Give yourself a break, and don't give up or give in to negativity! Good things take time, and you're getting there.

9. Remember, letting go of drama isn't about having the ability to forget the past; it's about having the wisdom and strength to embrace the present.

10. The single greatest problem in communication is the illusion that it has taken place.

11. Too often we don't listen to understand—we listen to reply. Don't do this. Focus. Be curious. When you listen with genuine curiosity, you don't listen with the intent to reply—you listen for what's truly behind the words.

12. When you hear only what you want to hear, you're not really listening. Listen to what you don't want to hear too. That's how we grow stronger, together.

13. You never know what someone has been through today. So don't make empty judgments about them or their situation. Be kind. Be teachable. Be a good friend. Be a good neighbor. Be a good listener.

14. Sometimes all a person needs is an empathetic ear—they just need to know someone else hears them. Simply offering a listening ear and a kind heart for their suffering can be incredibly healing.

15. Do not make judgments unless you undoubtedly know the whole story. If in doubt, ask the person directly until you have clarity.

16. When you take the time to actually listen, with humility, to what people have to say, it's amazing what you can learn. Especially if the people doing the talking happen to be people you love.

17. Inner peace and harmony begin the moment you take a deep breath and choose not to allow another person or event to control your thoughts and emotions.

18. Even when your frustration is justified, and something needs to be said, don't be hateful—keep your heart and mind wide open. Peace is not the absence of trouble, but the presence of love. Be mindful, and communicate accordingly.

19. It's much easier to overreact and judge people than it is to understand them. Understanding takes extra kindness and patience. And this

"extra" is what love is all about. Love is living your life . . . but sharing it. It's forgiveness, patience, and optimism, and sometimes it's a hug or a smile when there's nothing left to say.

20. Keep doing your best not to overthink life's little frustrations and disagreements. Answers come to a relaxed mind. Space allows things to fall into place. A good attitude yields the best results in the end.

Put On Your Own Oxygen Mask First

HERE'S A FAMILIAR scene: You're driving home and someone gives you the middle finger. What do you do? Honk and give the finger back and cuss out loud in the car?

That's the easy response.

But when we combat toxicity and negativity by being toxic and negative right back, we feed the situation rather than help it.

So what's the better response? Take a three-second pause, take a deep breath, breathe in, breathe out, and ask yourself, "How can I respond in a kind, loving, caring, compassionate way?"

We know it's easier said than done, but it can be done. We have found that the first approach to dealing with toxicity and negativity in our lives is to distinguish between two types of toxic or negative people so that we are better able to cope with them effectively. Depending on the person and the situation, the negativity is either acute or chronic.

It's acute if someone is hurting or dealing with a major life change that's thrown them off-kilter. Either way, there's a reason or cause for them acting the way they are. It's chronic if someone is always a negative drain; no matter whether they are struggling or not, it's part of their personality complex. It might be a family member, and you can't distance yourself from the person's constant complaining or negativity.

Regardless of whether someone in your life is acutely or chronically toxic, the only way that you can diffuse the situation or support the individual who's suffering is to be in a good place yourself. If you enter a situation with angst, anger, stress, or frustration, or lacking presence, you are going to spew more venom and end up being another source of toxicity.

We've been in the familiar situation we started this chapter with, where we're driving and someone else on the road goes crazy. If we're in a place of taking care of ourselves, do you know what happens? The other person honks or gives us the finger, and we just laugh. It doesn't affect us to the point of responding with anger or hatred. We are in a good place ourselves, and so we can set a boundary for ourselves, realizing that we don't need to worry about this other person. We can laugh at it and let it roll off our shoulders because we are not internalizing the negativity coming at us.

In other more difficult situations with people we care about, when, whether acute or chronic, their toxicity is creating stress and negativity in their life that is in turn being spewed at us, we need to be in a place where we can handle the hard stuff more effectively. That doesn't mean to the point of laughing it off, but instead working toward a more peaceful response for ourselves and for the other person.

For example, Angel has a friend who lost her husband because of an unexpected heart failure. The conversations and meals that Angel has shared with this friend have been incredibly emotional and heavy. These times haven't been easy—understandably so when helping a friend work through grief. And Angel, being empathetic, absorbs some of the negative emotional pain. But while she's making herself available to support her friend, she is also taking care of herself with time to meditate, practice yoga, go to the float studio, or simply relax. By doing those things, she is better able to support her friend when they spend time together.

You can be a source of compassion, and you can go above and beyond for others, but that doesn't mean nonstop. Focus on the people in your life who matter, while setting the necessary boundaries so that you protect and replenish your time and energy. When you support someone at a deep level of acute negativity because of a painful loss or other life change, remember to put your own oxygen mask on first.

9 Rampant Toxic Behaviors That Tear Relationships Apart

Our behavior is a small thing that makes a big difference in our relationships.

ONE MORNING WE saw a middle-aged woman ferociously slam the car door in her husband's face and storm off into a department store. Then, an hour later, we noticed two twentysomething friends sitting next to us at a local coffee shop, the man staring down at his iPhone the entire time his friend shared with him her concerns about her sister's drug addiction. And then we came across someone's rant on Facebook about their significant other that concluded with "ALL MEN are exactly the same!"

Most of us have likely done something similar in our relationships at some point, because relationships aren't easy, and sometimes we make missteps. In fact, let's be honest: We've all acted in toxic, damaging ways at one time or another. None of us are immune to occasional toxic mood swings. But that doesn't excuse what we do to each other.

With practice, we *can* do better.

Over the years, through our coaching practice, Getting Back to Happy course, and live events, we have worked with thousands of individuals and couples looking to fix their failing relationships, and we've learned a lot about what it takes to make this happen. One of the most significant realizations is the fact that most failing and failed relationships (both intimate and platonic) suffer from the same basic behavioral issues. We're sharing them here in hopes that doing so will help you catch yourself in the act, so you can course-correct when necessary.

The Big Four

Believe it or not, roughly 90 percent of the failing relationships we've witnessed over the years suffered from one or more of the following:

1. Using complaints and disagreements as an opportunity to condemn each other

Complaints are okay. Disagreements are okay too. These are natural, honest reactions to a person's decisions or behavior. But when complaints and disagreements spiral out of control into global attacks on the person, and not on their decisions or behavior, this spells trouble. Remember, there's a big difference between who someone *is* and what they sometimes *do*.

2. Using hateful gestures as a substitute for honest communication

Remember that frequent name-calling, threats, eye-rolling, belittling, mockery, hostile teasing, etc.—in whatever form, gestures like these are poisonous to a relationship because they convey hate. And it's virtually impossible to resolve a relationship problem when the other person is constantly receiving the message that you hate them.

Keep in mind that if someone you love makes a mistake and you choose to forgive them, your actions must reinforce your words. In other words, let bygones be bygones. Don't use their past wrongdoings to justify your present righteousness. When you constantly use someone's past wrongdoings to make yourself seem "better" than them ("I'm better than you because, unlike you, I didn't do X, Y, Z in the past"), it's a lose-lose situation.

Replace your negative thoughts with positive communication! Because the truth is, if you're throwing hateful gestures at a person instead of communicating with them, there's a good chance they don't even know why you're being so mean. When communication between two people isn't open and honest, there's a lot of important stuff that never gets said.

3. Denying responsibility for your role in the relationship

When you deny responsibility in every relationship dispute, all you're really doing is blaming the other person. You're saying, in effect, "The problem here is never me, and it's always you." This denial of accountability escalates every argument, because there's a complete and utter breakdown of communication.

The key thing to understand is that you have a choice. Either you're choosing to be in a relationship with another person, or you aren't. If you're choosing to be in a relationship, then you are responsible for it. Denying this means you're giving up all your power to the other person—you're their victim, regardless of circumstances (positive or negative), because you've given them 100 percent of the responsibility for the relationship you have with them.

So remember, even when the behavior driving a relationship dispute belongs to the other person, the only way to find common ground, or simply to create more healthy space for yourself, is to first own the fact that you are 50 percent responsible for the relationship at all times. Once you do, you have the power to make progress one way or the other.

4. Giving the silent treatment

Remember that tuning out, ignoring, disengaging, refusing to acknowledge, etc.—any variation of the silent treatment doesn't just remove the other person from the argument you're having with them; it ends up removing them, emotionally, from the relationship you have with them.

When you're ignoring someone, you're really teaching them to live without you. If that's what you want, be clear about it. And if not, drop it!

Five More Worth Avoiding

Although not quite as prevalent as the four mentioned above, these behavioral issues are still incredibly common relationship-killers:

5. Using emotional blackmail

Emotional blackmail happens when you apply an emotional penalty against someone if they don't do exactly what you want them to do. The key condition here is that they change their behavior, against their will, as a result of the emotional blackmail. In other words, absent the emotional blackmail they would live differently, but they fear the penalty—or punishment—and so they give in. This is an extremely unhealthy relationship behavior.

The solution, again, relies heavily on better communication. There should *not* be a penalty, just an honest conversation. If two people care about each other and want to maintain a healthy relationship, they absolutely need to be "allowed" to openly communicate *all* their feelings to each other—their true feelings—not just the agreeable and positive ones. If this is not "allowed" or supported by one or both people involved in the relationship—if one or both people fear punishment for their honesty—lies and deceit will gradually replace love and trust, which ultimately leads to a complete emotional disconnection.

6. Withholding the truth

Trust is the bedrock of a healthy relationship, and when trust is broken, it takes a long time and commitment on the part of both parties involved to repair it and heal. The key thing to remember here is that secrets can be just as deceitful as openly telling a lie.

All too often, we'll hear one of our students say something like, "I didn't tell him, but I didn't lie about it either." This statement is a contradiction, as omissions are lies. If you're covering up your tracks or withholding the truth in any way, it's only a matter of time before the truth comes out and trust in the relationship completely breaks down. So speak the truth, always.

Being honest is the only way to be at peace with yourself and those you care about.

7. Putting each other on the back burner

Failing to carve out quality time for your important relationships is one of the most unhealthy relationship mistakes of them all, and yet it often flies under the radar . . . at least for a while . . . until everything begins to fall apart.

The truth is, relationships are like every other living entity in the sense that they require nurturing in order to survive and thrive. It's easy to allow the rush of our busy lives to take over, especially when we have young children, work, hobbies, friends, and a body that demands nourishing food and regular exercise. But your relationship with someone is a body as well, and if it's not nourished with quality time every week, it will start to wither.

Dedicate ample time every week to focus exclusively on those you care about. Nothing you can give is more appreciated than your sincere, focused attention—your full presence. Being with someone, listening without a ticking clock and without anticipation of the next scheduled event, is the ultimate compliment.

8. Needing or expecting your relationship to always be easy

When your marriage, friendship, or parenting gets difficult, it's not an immediate sign that you're doing it wrong. These intimate, intricate relationships are toughest when you're doing them right—when you're dedicating time, having the tough conversations, and making daily sacrifices.

Healthy, long-term relationships are amazing, but rarely easy 24/7. Resisting the hard times and seeing them as immediate evidence that something is wrong or that you're with the wrong person only exacerbates the difficulties. By contrast, finding the patience and mindfulness to view the challenges as an opportunity to work together will give your relationship the energy and strength needed to transcend the problems and grow even stronger in the long run.

9. Expecting your relationship to solve all your personal problems

It's easy to believe that it's your partner's or best friend's job to make you feel happy and whole. But the truth is, while a healthy relationship can bring tremendous delight to your life, it's not their responsibility to fill in your empty voids. That's your responsibility and yours alone, and until you accept this responsibility (for your unhappiness, frustration, boredom, etc.), problems will inevitably continue in your relationship.

Another way of looking at this is to realize that healthy relationships contain two people who practice self-care as individuals. When two people meet, the biggest prize always goes to the one with the most self-acceptance. He or she will be calmer, more confident, and more at ease with the other person. Truth be told, what you see in the mirror is often what you see in your relationships. Your petty disappointments in your partner and friends often reflect your petty disappointments in yourself. Your acceptance of your partner or friends often reflects your acceptance of yourself. Thus, the first step to having a truly healthy, long-term relationship with someone else is to have a healthy relationship with yourself.

Once You Understand the Toxic Behaviors, Remember . . .

The way we treat people we disagree with is a report card on what we've learned about love, compassion, acceptance, and kindness.

Sadly, some people waste years in a relationship trying to change the other person's mind, even though this usually can't be done, because many of the disagreements they have with this person are rooted in fundamental differences of opinion, personality, or values. By fighting over these deep-seated differences, all they succeed in doing is wasting their time and running their relationship into the ground.

So how do people in healthy relationships deal with issues that can't be resolved?

As mentioned earlier in this book, they accept one another as is. These people understand that problems are an inevitable part of any long-term relationship, in the same way chronic physical difficulties are inevitable as we grow older and wiser. These problems are like a weak knee or a bad back—we may not want these problems, but we're able to cope with them, to avoid situations that irritate them, and to develop strategies that help us deal with them.

Psychologist Dan Wile said it best in his book *After the Honeymoon*: "When choosing to engage yourself in a long-term relationship, you will inevitably be choosing a particular set of unsolvable problems that you'll be grappling with for the next 10, 20 or 50 years."

Bottom line: The best relationships are the best not because they have always been the happiest, but because they have stayed strong through the mightiest of storms.

Therefore, it's crucial to understand and alleviate the toxic behaviors we've discussed above. And then consciously remind yourself that . . .

Acceptance of one another is of vital importance to every relationship.

In the end, how you make others feel about themselves says a whole lot about you. So treat people right. Your love, compassion, acceptance, and kindness are gifts you can always afford to give.

IF YOU CAN relate to any of these toxic behaviors, remember that you are not alone. We all have unhealthy personalities buried deep within us that have the potential to occasionally sneak up on us and those closest to us. As mentioned above, **the key is awareness—recognizing these toxic behaviors and then course-correcting when necessary.**

10 Signs Your Friend Is Toxic

TOXIC FRIENDS COMPLICATE your life. These people are more than a nuisance; they're parasitic. Precious time slips away as you deal with their negativity, and you're left wondering why you feel so despondent. If you're ready to simplify your life, you can't condone these toxic friendships any longer.

What Toxic Friends Do

1. They drain you. You feel psychologically and emotionally depleted after spending time with them, instead of uplifted.

2. They are unsupportive. You're afraid to tell them about new, important aspects of your life because they've been unsupportive or downright rude about your ideas in the past.

3. They are up to no good. They regularly partake in activities that are morally unjust.

4. Their values and interests are opposite to your own. Dissimilar value systems often mix like oil and water. This doesn't necessarily mean the other person is wrong; it just means they aren't right for you.

5. They are unreliable. They always break their promises.

6. They contact you only when they need something. Otherwise you never hear from them.

7. They aren't meeting you halfway. If you are always the one calling your friends to make plans and going out of your way to be with them, but they never return the favor and attempt to go out of their way for you, there's a problem.

8. They are jealous of you. Jealousy is "I want what you have, and I want to take it away from you."

9. They have zero ambition. Beware: A lack of ambition can be contagious. As the saying goes, "You can't soar like an eagle when you hang out with turkeys."

10. They constantly drive you to moments of insanity. You catch yourself daydreaming about how good it would feel to throw a banana cream pie in their face.

Our Story of Toxicity

Here's why we know how bad these friendships can be: We've been on both sides of the court. Yeah, we have our share of victim stories about friends who were friends only if we agreed with them and gave them the spotlight. We've got tales of woe about past friends who were fabulous and fun, provided we didn't try to cut into their time by (gasp!) spending time alone and having other friendships. (You know, having a life outside of them?)

But the truth is that we've also been terrible friends at times, and we realize this. In the past we have neglected some friendships by relying on the other person to stay in touch instead of being the ones to reach out. Some of these friendships withered away over time because of our toxic behavior. Bottom line: Toxicity is a two-way street—you have to be a good friend too. (Hold this thought; we'll come back to it.)

How to End a Toxic Friendship

In our experience, there are two ways to end a toxic friendship: quickly and painfully or slowly and awkwardly. Neither is fun, neither is neat, and neither is easy.

If you still want to keep this person in your life, but to a lesser degree:

- **Stop responding to fake crisis calls.** If you don't drop everything to take their "I'm so devastated! My boss gave me a look that I think means he secretly hates me and that jerk from marketing wore the same shirt as me" calls, they'll find someone else who will. Or they'll deal with it. Either way, it's okay to step back and get off the first-alert list for calling in nonemergencies.
- **Take positive control of negative conversations.** It's okay to change the topic, talk about you, or steer conversations away from pity parties and self-absorbed sagas. Be willing to disagree with them and deal with the consequences.
- **Demonstrate that you won't be insulted or belittled.** To be honest, we've never had much luck trying to call toxic people out when

they've insulted us. The best response we've gotten is, "I'm sorry you took what I said so personally." Much more effective has been ending conversations with sickening sweetness or just plain abruptness. The message is clear: There is no reward for subtle digs and no games will be played at your end.

- **Be brutally honest.** Some people really don't recognize their own toxic tendencies or their inconsiderate behavior. You can actually tell a person, "I feel like you ignore me until you need something." You can also be honest if their overly negative attitude is what's driving you away: "I'm trying to focus on positive things. What's something good that we can talk about?" It may work or it may not, but your honesty will ensure that any friendship that continues forward is built on mutually beneficial ground.

If you want to completely end your relationship with the person in question:

- **Stop taking their calls completely.** If you're stuck seeing them on a regular basis—if for example, it's a coworker—keep things on a purely professional level. Find a reason to leave and excuse yourself as needed. It's passive-aggressive to expect avoidance to handle the problem, but it's an important component. You can't cut ties if you still chat on a regular basis.
- **Firmly tell them you've had enough.** If you've decided it's time to cut a truly toxic influence out of your life, you can let them know honestly (without being cruel). "I just can't be friends with you right now" isn't fun to hear, but it has the benefit of putting everybody on the same page.
- **Make new friends worth having.** Seriously! Give your time to friends you connect with and enjoy. The long shadows of toxic

friends shrink considerably when you've got better things to do with your time than worry about their negativity.

Finally, Be a Good Friend

It doesn't help to cut toxic friends out of your life if you're not ready to foster quality friendships. On occasion, you may find that the toxicity of a friendship drains away when you start being a better friend yourself.

Make that first call, offer a genuine compliment, schedule a fun outing with another person in mind, send that ridiculously funny card for no real reason—there are tons of ways to nurture your friendships. When you're surrounded by good friends and good intentions, it's amazing how pettiness and toxicity simply evaporate.

12 Negative Thoughts That Push People Away from You

IN OUR LINE of work, we hear from hundreds of coaching clients and students enrolled in our Getting Back to Happy course every month. Through this experience, we often see the same exact negative thinking patterns tearing otherwise healthy individuals apart. And we've witnessed firsthand the devastation this negativity causes to their personal and professional growth, and to their relationships.

But let's be honest, we all get our minds stuck in the gutter sometimes. None of us are immune to the negative thoughts that creep up in the backs of our minds. However, that doesn't mean we have to succumb to them. Whether your negative thinking is a common occurrence or just a once-in-a-while phenomenon, it's critical for your long-term happiness and success that you are able to recognize when you're thinking negatively and then consciously shift your mindset from negative to positive.

Here are twelve of the most common negative thoughts we see people struggle with, and some tips to get back on track:

1. "I need to be exactly who they want me to be." Life offers you a priceless opportunity in every single moment to see and experience Who You Really Are. Seize it! Sometimes we get completely lost in trying to live life for others, trying to meet their expectations, doing things just to impress them. Take a moment now and stop yourself. Are you doing things because you truly believe in them? Remember your own needs and goals. Remember who *you* are. Live, do, and love so that you are happy too, because when it comes down to it, you can't be true to others unless you are true to yourself first.

2. "I don't like them, because they are different." Make a promise to yourself. Promise to stop the drama before it begins, to breathe deeply and peacefully, and to love others and yourself without conditions. Promise to laugh at your own mistakes, and to realize that no one is perfect; we are all human. Feelings of self-worth can flourish only in an atmosphere where individual differences are appreciated, mistakes are tolerated, communication is open, and rules are flexible.

3. "They have it so much easier than I do." No one has it easier than you. Every one of us is fighting our own private battles. The strongest among us aren't those who show strength we can see, but those who have won incredible inner battles we know nothing about. Assuming someone has it easier than you do only builds a barrier between the two of you.

4. "I don't have enough (or I am not enough) to make a difference." Many of your greatest accomplishments in life will come when you are able to bless someone else while you are going through your own storm. So regardless of what's going on in your life, be gentle and kind. Think before you speak and act. Always remember that the words and actions you choose can only be forgiven, not forgotten. You were made to make a difference, so embrace every opportunity to do so. No act of your kindness, no matter how tiny, will ever be wasted.

5. "I am a victim here and there's nothing I can do about it." Another toxic train of thought is one that fuels a sense of victimization. Believing that you're a victim, that you have no power to exert and no power over the direction of your life, is a toxic stance that keeps you stuck. Working as life coaches with people who have suffered major trauma but found the courage to turn it all around, we know we all have access to far more power, authority, and influence over our lives than we initially believe. When you stop complaining and refuse to see yourself as a helpless victim, you'll find that you are more powerful than you realized, but only if you choose to accept this reality.

6. "It's all their fault." If you sit around for too long blaming others for the things they did or didn't do, or know or didn't know, you'll remain sitting in one spot forever. Placing blame is easy, because it means you don't have to do anything; you just have to sit around for your entire life. But that's not living; that's dying. To accept where you are without blame by seizing the present for what it is—for the opportunities it's giving you every instant—that's what injects life into your story, into your relationships, and ultimately moves you forward.

7. "I will never forgive them." We often keep our hearts closed, not because we don't trust others not to leave us, let us down, or stop loving us, but because we don't trust ourselves to survive the pain of them leaving, letting us down, or not loving us anymore. How ironic, considering that only by suffering through these very losses do we come to realize our true strength. Truth be told, it takes a strong heart to love, but it takes an even stronger heart to continue to love after it's been hurt. If someone hurts you, betrays you, or breaks your heart, forgive them, for they have helped you learn about trust and the importance of being cautious when you open your heart. You are stronger now and better equipped to find the kind of love you deserve. Bottom line: Don't let the wrong people from your past keep you from the right people in your present. Forgive and move forward.

8. "They deserve my cruelty." One of the most toxic behaviors—cruelty—stems from a total lack of empathy, concern, or compassion for others. We see it every day online and in the media—people being devastatingly unkind and hurtful to others just because they can. They tear people down online in a cowardly way, using their anonymity as a shield. Cruelty, backstabbing, and hurting others for any reason is toxic, and it hurts you as well. If you find yourself backstabbing and tearing someone else down, stop in your tracks. Dig deep and find compassion in your heart, and realize that we're all in this together.

9. "I'm way too busy for family and friends right now." The people you take for granted today may be the only ones you need tomorrow. Never be too busy to make time for those who matter most, because sooner or later you just want to be around those special people who make you smile. So today, make time for those who help you love yourself more. Schedule them into your busy day. They are worth it.

10. "It's okay to stretch the truth sometimes." No, it really isn't. In fact, it's disheartening to think how many people are shocked by honesty, and how few by deceit. Don't be one of them. Uphold the truth always. Those who are easily shocked should be shocked more often, and you should be the one shocking them with honest words and deeds every day. The bottom line here is that an honest, loving heart is the beginning of everything that is right with this world. It's what brings us together and keeps us together through thick and thin.

11. "My mistakes today prove that I am a failure." This mindset will drive you and everyone around you crazy. Finish each day and be done with it. You have done the best you could. Some blunders and absurdities no doubt crept in; forgive and forget them as soon as you can. Remember, your failure does not define you; your determination does. Failure is simply the opportunity to begin again, smarter than before. Tomorrow is a new day. You shall begin it peacefully and with too high a spirit to be encumbered with old nonsense.

12. "It needs to be perfect before I can move forward." As human beings, we often chase hypothetical, static states of perfection. We do so when we are searching for the perfect house, job, friend, or lover. The problem, of course, is that perfection doesn't exist in a static state. Because life is a continual journey, constantly evolving and changing. What is here today will not be exactly the same tomorrow—that perfect house, job, friend, or lover will eventually fade to a state of imperfection. But with a little patience and an open mind, over time that imperfect house evolves into a comfortable home. That imperfect job evolves into a rewarding career. That imperfect friend evolves into a steady shoulder to lean on. And that imperfect lover evolves into a reliable lifelong companion. It's just a matter of letting perfectionism *go*.

12 Truths That Will Bring Peace When You Deal with Difficult People

IF YOU'VE BEEN feeling drained by your regular encounters with a difficult person, we urge you to gradually implement and practice the strategies we've outlined above, one at a time. Then, as you're doing this, proactively remind yourself *not* to engage in this person's negative behavior. Don't get sucked in. Keep your composure. Keep your inner peace.

Do so by reading the following truths to yourself daily, until they become deeply rooted in your consciousness.

1. The greatest stress you go through when dealing with a difficult person is not fueled by the words or actions of this person; it is fueled by your mind giving their words and actions importance.

2. It's okay to be upset. It's never okay to be cruel. Rage, hate, resentment, and jealousy do not change the hearts of others—they only change yours.

3. Forgive others, not because they deserve forgiveness, but because you deserve peace. Free yourself of the burden of being an eternal victim.

4. Stay positive when negativity surrounds you. Smile when others refuse to. It's an easy way to make a difference in the world around you.

5. Gossip and drama end at a wise person's ears. Be wise. Seek to understand before you attempt to judge. Use your judgment not as a weapon for putting others down, but as a tool for making positive choices that help you build your own character.

6. Always set an example. Treat everyone with kindness and respect, even those who are rude to you—not because they are nice, but because *you* are. And do your best to be thankful for rude and difficult people too—they serve as great reminders of how not to be.

7. The way we treat people we strongly disagree with is a report card on what we've learned about love, compassion, and kindness. Life is too short to argue and fight. Count your blessings, value the people who matter, and move on from the drama with your head held high.

8. Don't expect to see positive changes in your life if you constantly surround yourself with difficult people. The great danger of being around difficult people too often is that you start to become like them without even knowing it. So be mindful of the daily company you keep. (Just because you are kind and respectful to someone, does *not* mean you have to spend extra time with them.)

9. Remember that what others say and do and the opinions they have are based almost entirely on their own self-reflection. Don't take things personally. Instead of getting angry over the words of others, choose to be mindful and choose to grow stronger, one way or the other, because of them.

10. Let the opinions of others inform you . . . don't let them limit you. Don't let anyone's ignorance, hate, drama, or negativity stop you from being the best person you can be. If you find yourself constantly trying to prove your worth to others, you've already forgotten your value. Take a deep breath, and do what you know is right.

11. If you really want to be happy and peaceful, then stop being afraid of being yourself, and stop thinking about what others think of you every second. There's nothing selfish about giving yourself enough space for self-care. We can't give what we don't have. Experience life on your terms and you'll be life-giving to others.

12. Make it a daily ritual to work hard in silence, to do what you have to do, and to ignore the drama, discouragement, and negativity surrounding you. Let your success be your noise in the end.

CONFLICT & DRAMA QUESTIONS TO MAKE *YOU* THINK

What do you try to keep in mind when a relationship gets rough?

How has needless drama affected you and your relationships?

What negative behaviors interfere with your relationships?

How have difficult people, or difficult relationship issues, affected you in recent times?

How has your negativity pushed people away from you?

What are the limiting beliefs you have been living by that have affected your relationship?

Why did your relationship break down?

Where can you take responsibility?

How is this conflict affecting your mental well-being?

Why is this conflict important to you?

PART SIX

Boundaries & Expectations

Learn to Accept What Is

BOUNDARIES AND EXPECTATIONS are a big part of cultivating healthy relationships, and they go hand-in-hand. When we expect others—or even ourselves—to behave a certain way, it ends up causing a lot of pain.

Here's an example from our life. When our son, Mac, was first born, Angel thought she would immediately be the perfect mom and still be able to work with no trouble. And, of course, her expectations of what a mother looked like was inaccurate. When she pictured what her life would look like as a new mom and a business owner, needless to say, Angel's expectations got the best of her.

To overcome this, she had to set boundaries for herself. She set boundaries to determine when she'd be working and when she'd be with Mac. During her working hours, it was time to be productive on business items and not worry about planning playdates or anything else related to her responsibilities as a mom. During her time with Mac, she would be fully present with him and not think about work or her responsibilities as a business owner.

She struggled at first, because when she was working, she thought she should be with Mac. And when she was with Mac, she felt guilty because she thought she should be working. Establishing the boundaries helped her to be flexible, make adjustments, reevaluate her expectations, and accept what life would be like for us now with a son.

Of course, we experience issues with expectations and boundaries in other aspects of our lives, especially when it comes to other people, and in particular our family relationships. Family members are people who, at least subconsciously, we often hold to a higher standard that, in many cases, is unreasonable. We do it on a daily basis because these are the people who are closest to us. We assume—and expect—that because they love us, they should treat us a certain way at all times. We've known these people our whole lives; we know exactly who they are, so therefore they should always behave according to the standard in our head.

The reality is that they have their own issues. They are individuals with their own ebbs and flows of emotions, problems, and everything else that life brings along, which means that who we know them to be in our head is not always the person in front of us at any given moment under certain circumstances. Unfortunately, it's also very rare that we expect less of others than what they give. We're always expecting more, so they let us down constantly.

But they are not letting us down. It's our expectations that let us down.

The expectations that we have created cause us to overlook the reality of our own family's situation, and for some reason the rules that apply to friends and those outside our inner circle are different from the rules that apply to family and people who are a part of the inner circle. We have to work to check the expectations and set boundaries so that we can extend the same compassion and patience to those we love the most.

The recurring theme here is that the thing we can control is our expectations, and that has absolutely nothing to do with other people or family members we perceive to be letting us down—again, based on the standards we've created in our own head. If we can instead practice accepting what is—to be patient, present, and happy with what we have, knowing that everything has happened as it should—we can then take a positive step forward. Remember, positivity is not about always expecting the best outcome; it's accepting what does happen and making the best of it.

Where Happiness Is Found: The Stories Too Many People Believe for Too Long

A Wondrous Place

When we shared a story about letting go of expectations with a small group of VIP attendees at our most recent Think Better, Live Better conference, a woman named Annie raised her hand and said (we're sharing this with permission):

"I can honestly relate in the most profound way."

"My husband suffered a head injury in 2014 that wiped away his long-term lifetime memories. He doesn't remember anything before summer of that year, including our past. He did, however, know he loved me. It was like an innate knowing. The same as his passions, which have remained as they were before his injury, even though he couldn't tell you anything about how he pursued them before 2014.

"At fifty years old, my husband has only four years of 'stories,' and I have seen this turn him into a very happy man. He invents himself a day at a time. He has a childlike quality, as in eagerness and appreciation, that is inspiring to be around. I think he embodies the 'story-free world,' and I can attest to what a wondrous place it is."

Then, as a group, we discussed Annie's experience and openly practiced questioning our own stories and letting them go. Here's the basic gist of what we practiced together:

Letting Go of Your Story

First and foremost, it's important to understand that many of the biggest misunderstandings in life could be avoided if we simply took the time to ask, "What else could this mean?" A wonderful and practical way to do this is by using a reframing tool we initially picked up from research professor Brené Brown, which we then tailored through our coaching work with students and conference attendees. We call the tool "The Story I'm Telling Myself." Although asking the question itself—"What else could this mean?"—can help reframe our thoughts and broaden our perspectives, using the simple phrase "The story I'm telling myself is" as a prefix to troubling thoughts has undoubtedly created many aha moments for our students and conference attendees in recent times.

Here's how it works: "The story I'm telling myself" tool can be applied to any difficult life situation or circumstance in which a troubling thought is getting the best of you. For example, perhaps someone you love (husband, wife, boyfriend, girlfriend, etc.) didn't call you on their lunch break when they said they would, and now an hour has passed and you're feeling upset because you're obviously not a high-enough priority to them. So when you catch yourself feeling this way, use the phrase "The story I'm telling myself is that they didn't call me because I'm not a high-enough priority to them."

Then ask yourself these questions:

- Can I be absolutely certain this story is true?
- How do I feel and behave when I tell myself this story?
- What's one other possibility that might also make the ending to this story true?

Give yourself the space to think it all through carefully. Challenge yourself to think differently! "The story I'm telling myself" and the three related questions give you tools for revisiting and reframing the troubling or confusing situations that arise in your daily life. From there, you can challenge the stories you subconsciously tell yourself and do a reality check with a more objective mindset.

This will ultimately allow you to let go of the stories that aren't serving you and the people you love.

6 Incredibly Common Reasons We Become Our Own Worst Enemies

Inner peace begins the moment you take a deep breath and choose not to allow another person or event to control your thoughts.

FOR THE LONGEST time Marc had tunnel vision and expected life to be a certain way. He studied his failures until he lost sight of his successes. He surrendered his dreams to feel a sense of comfort. He crafted limiting beliefs and shielded himself from love and happiness by refusing to put himself out there. And as he did all this, he sat back and wondered why life was so miserable.

Obviously, he was very lost.

Marc began to turn things around about a decade ago when his stubborn habits led him into a chaotic argument with Angel. As we both stared at each other through tears, Angel said, "Marc, you are the enemy—your enemy. It's your choices. I can't sympathize any longer. You can choose differently if you want to, but you have to want to. Please want to!" And after some extensive soul-searching, lots of reading, a little sabbatical, and continuous support from a loving wife and a few close friends, Marc learned to choose differently and eventually found himself again.

We tell you this because we know you struggle with similar inner demons—occasionally we all do. Sometimes our thoughts and routine choices are our biggest enemies. Which is why we want to remind you to beware of . . .

1. The expectation of constant contentment

Nothing in life is constant. There is neither absolute happiness nor absolute sadness. There are only the changes in our moods that continuously oscillate between these two extremes.

At any given moment we are comparing how we currently feel to how we felt at another time—comparing one level of our contentment to another. In this way, those of us who have felt great sadness are best able to feel heightened feelings of happiness after we emotionally heal. In other words, happiness and sadness need each other. One reinforces the other. Humans must know misery to identify times of elation.

The key is to focus on the good. May you live each moment of your life consciously, and realize that all the happiness you seek is present if you are prepared to notice it. If you are willing to appreciate that this moment is far better than it could have been, you will enjoy it more for what it truly is.

2. The obsession with examining personal failures

Imagine being enrolled in five college classes in which you achieved one A, two Bs, and two Cs. Would you concentrate on the A or the Cs? Would you berate yourself for falling short in the C classes? Or would you capitalize on your obvious interest and aptitude in the subject matter of the A class? We hope you realize the value of the latter. While you might want to improve in the C classes, berating yourself is not a healthy path forward. And the A classes might shine some light on where your innate talents and passions lie.

Every morning when you wake up, think of three things that are going well in your life at the moment. As you fall asleep every night, fill your mind with an appreciation for all the small things that went well during the day. Examine your successes.

Give the power of your thinking to the positive influences in your life, and they will grow stronger and more influential every day. Remind yourself often of what works well and why, and you'll naturally find ways to make lots of other things work well too. The most efficient way to enjoy more success in life is not to obsess yourself with what hasn't worked in the past, but instead to extend and expand upon the success you already know.

3. The urge to surrender to the draw of comfort

The most common and destructive addiction in the world is the draw of comfort. Why pursue growth when you already have four hundred television channels and a recliner? Just pass the chip dip and lose yourself in a trance. *Wrong!* That's not living—that's existing. Living is about learning and growing through excitement and discomfort.

Life is filled with questions, many of which don't have an obvious or immediate answer. It's your willingness to ask these questions, and your courage to march confidently into the unknown in search of the answers, that gives life its meaning.

In the end, you can spend your life feeling sorry for yourself, cowering in the comfort of your routines, wondering why there are so many problems out in the real world, or you can be thankful that you are strong enough to endure them. It just depends on your mindset. The obvious first step, though, is convincing yourself to step out of your comfort zone.

4. The self-limiting beliefs

You do not suffer from your beliefs. You suffer from your disbeliefs. If you have no hope inside you, it's not because there is no hope; it's because you don't believe there is.

Since the mind drives the body, it's the way you think that eventually makes the dreams you dream possible or impossible. Your reality is simply a reflection of your thoughts and the way you routinely contemplate what you know to be true. All too often we literally do not know any better than good enough. Sometimes you have to try to do what you think you can't do so that you realize that you actually *can*.

It all starts on the inside. You control your thoughts. The only person who can hold you down is *you*.

5. The resistance to being vulnerable

Love is vulnerability. Happiness is vulnerability. The risk of being vulnerable is the price of opening yourself to beauty and opportunity.

Being vulnerable is not about showing the parts of you that are polished; it's about revealing the unpolished parts you would rather keep hidden from the world. It's about looking out into the world with an honest, open heart and saying, "This is me. Take me or leave me."

It's hard to consciously choose vulnerability. Why? Because the stakes are high. If you reveal your authentic self, there is the possibility that you will be misunderstood, judged, or even rejected. The fear of these things is so powerful that you put on an armored mask to protect yourself. But, of course, this only perpetuates the pain you are trying to avoid.

The truth is that nothing worthwhile in this world is a safe bet. Since love and happiness are born out of your willingness to be vulnerable—to be open to something wonderful that could be taken away from you—when you hide from your vulnerability, you automatically hide from everything in life worth attaining.

6. The expectations of how things are supposed to be

There's this fantasy in your head about how you think things are supposed to be. This fantasy blinds you from reality and prevents you from appreciating the genuine goodness that exists in your life.

The solution? Simple: Drop the needless expectations. Appreciate what is. Hope for the best, but expect less.

You have to accept reality instead of fighting it. Don't let what you expected to happen blind you from all the good things that are happening. When you stop expecting people and things to be perfectly the way you had imagined, you can enjoy them for who and what they truly are.

Afterthoughts

Today, do your best to leverage the reminders above. The overarching goal is to gradually change your response to what you can't control. To grow so strong on the inside that nothing on the outside can affect your inner wellness without your conscious permission.

7 Things You Should Stop Expecting from Others

THE BIGGEST DISAPPOINTMENTS in our lives are often the result of misplaced expectations. This is especially true when it comes to our relationships and interactions with others.

Tempering your expectations of other people will greatly reduce unnecessary frustration and suffering, in both your life and theirs, and will help you refocus on the things that truly matter.

1. Stop expecting them to agree with you.

You deserve to be happy. You deserve to live a life you are excited about. Don't let the opinions of others make you forget that. You are not in this world to live up to the expectations of others, nor should you feel that others are here to live up to yours. In fact, the more you approve of your own decisions in life, the less approval you need from everyone else.

You have to dare to be yourself and follow you own intuition, however frightening or strange that may feel or prove to be. Don't compare yourself with others. Don't get discouraged by their progress or success. Follow your own path and stay true to your own purpose. Success is ultimately about spending your life happily in your own way.

2. Stop expecting them to respect you more than you respect yourself.

True strength is in the soul and spirit, not in muscles. It's about having faith and trust in who you are, and a willingness to act upon it. Decide this minute to never again beg anyone for the love, respect, and attention that you should be showing yourself.

Today, look at yourself in the mirror and say, "I love you, and from now on I'm going to act like it." It's important to be nice to others, but it's even more important to be nice to yourself. When you practice self-love and self-respect, you give yourself the opportunity to be happy. When you are happy, you become a better friend, a better family member, and a better *you*.

3. Stop expecting (and needing) them to like you.

You might feel unwanted and unworthy to one person, but you are priceless to another. Don't ever forget your worth. Spend time with those who value you. No matter how good you are to people, there will always be one negative person who criticizes you. Smile, ignore them, and carry on.

In this crazy world that's trying to make you the same as everyone else, the toughest battle you'll ever have to fight is the battle to be yourself. And as you're fighting back, not everyone will like you. Sometimes people will call you names because you're "different." But that's perfectly okay. The things that make you different are the things that make you, *you*, and the right people will love you for it.

4. Stop expecting them to fit your idea of who they are.

Loving and respecting others means allowing them to be themselves. When you stop expecting people to be a certain way, you can begin to appreciate *them*.

Pay close attention, and respect people for who they are and not for who you want them to be. We don't know most people half as well as we believe we do; and truly knowing someone is a big part of what makes them wonderful. Every human being is remarkable and beautiful; it just takes a patient set of eyes to see it. The more you get to know someone, the more you will be able to look beyond their appearance and see the beauty of who they truly are.

5. Stop expecting them to know what you're thinking.

People can't read minds. They will never know how you feel unless you tell them. Your boss? Yeah, he doesn't know you're hoping for a promotion, because you haven't told him yet. That cute guy you haven't talked to because you're too shy? Yeah, you guessed it—he hasn't given you the time of day simply because you haven't given him the time of day either.

In life, you have to communicate with others regularly and effectively. And often, you have to open your vocal cords and speak the first words. You have to tell people what you're thinking. It's as simple as that.

6. Stop expecting them to suddenly change.

You can't change people and you shouldn't try. Either you accept who they are or you choose to live without them. It might sound harsh, but it's not. When you try to change people, they often remain the same, but when you don't try to change them—when you support them and allow them the freedom to be as they are—they gradually change in the most beautiful way. Because what really changes is the way you see them.

7. Stop expecting them to be okay.

Be kinder than necessary, for everyone you meet is fighting some kind of battle, just like you are. Every smile or sign of strength hides an inner struggle every bit as complex and extraordinary as your own.

Remember that embracing your light doesn't mean ignoring your dark. We are measured by our ability to overcome adversities and insecurities, not by avoiding them. Supporting, sharing, and making contributions to other people is one of life's greatest rewards. This happens naturally if we allow it, because we all share very similar dreams, needs, and struggles. As mentioned earlier in this book, once we accept this, the world then is a place where we can look someone else in the eye and say, "I'm lost and struggling at the moment," and they can nod and say, "Me too," and that's okay. Because not being okay all the time is perfectly okay.

Afterthoughts

People rarely behave exactly the way you want them to. Again, hope for the best, but expect less. And remember, the magnitude of your happiness will be directly proportional to your thoughts and how you choose to think about things. Even if a situation or relationship doesn't work out, it's still worth it if it made you feel something new and if it taught you something new.

7 Ways to Protect Yourself from Other People's Negative Energy

It's tough to live a positive life around negative people.

DEALING WITH NEGATIVITY can be quite a downer. Angel once had a coworker whose negative energy would wash over her on a daily basis. In their conversations, the coworker would complain about everything—work tasks, family, friends, health, and anything else she could think of. She was also extremely cynical about others, often doubting their intentions and judging them harshly. Talking to her wasn't a pleasant experience, to say the least.

The first time Angel had a meeting with this coworker, she felt completely drained. It felt as if someone had sucked the life out of her, and it took a couple of hours for the effects to wear off. The same thing happened the next few times the two of them spoke too. Angel quickly realized she needed to work out an action plan to deal with this kind of negative energy.

Angel gradually developed several key strategies for dealing with negative people effectively. They have worked wonders in her life, and now we use them to assist hundreds of coaching and course students we interact with on a weekly basis. We hope you find value in them too.

1. Set and enforce limits.

Negative people who wallow in their problems and fail to focus on solutions are hard to deal with. They want people to join their 24/7 pity party so they can feel better about themselves. You may feel pressured to listen to their complaints simply because you don't want to be seen as callous or rude, but there's a fine line between lending a compassionate ear and getting sucked into their negative emotional drama.

You can avoid this drama by setting boundaries and distancing yourself when necessary. Think of it this way: If a negative person were chain-smoking cigarettes, would you sit beside them all day inhaling their secondhand smoke? No, you wouldn't—you'd distance yourself. So go ahead and give yourself some breathing room when you must.

If distancing yourself is impossible in the near term, another great way to set limits is to ask a negative person how they intend to fix the problem they're complaining about. Oftentimes they will either quiet down or redirect the conversation in a more harmonious direction, at least temporarily.

2. Respond mindfully—don't just react.

A reaction is a hot, thoughtless, in-the-moment eruption of emotion that's usually driven by your ego (as human beings, we're more likely to react when we're disconnected from our logical mind). It might last just a split second before your intuition kicks in and offers some perspective, or it might take over to the point that you act on it. When you feel angry or flustered after dealing with a negative person, that's a sign you've reacted rather than responded mindfully. Responding mindfully will leave you feeling like you handled things with integrity and poise.

Bottom line: When you encounter someone with a negative attitude, don't respond by throwing insults back at them. Keep your dignity and don't lower yourself to their level. True strength is being bold enough to walk away from the nonsense with your head held high.

3. Introduce lighter topics of discussion.

Some people's negative attitudes are triggered by specific, seemingly harmless topics. For example, one of Angel's friends turns into a self-victimizer whenever we talk about her job. No matter what Angel says, she'll complain about everything related to her job, and when Angel tries to interject with positive comments, she just rolls right over them with more negativity. Obviously this becomes quite a conversation dampener.

If you find yourself in a similar conversational situation, and the person you're talking with is stuck on a topic that's bringing either one of you down, realize their negative emotions may be too deeply rooted to address in a one-off conversation. Your best bet is to introduce a new topic to lighten the mood. Simple things like funny memories, mutual friendships, personal success stories, and other kinds of happy news make for light conversation. Keep it to areas the person feels positive about.

4. Focus on solutions, not problems.

Where and how you focus your attention determines your emotional state. When you zero in on the problems you're facing, you create and prolong negative emotions and stress. When you shift your focus toward actions that can improve your circumstances, you create a sense of self-efficacy that yields positive emotions and reduces stress.

The same exact principle applies when dealing with negative people—fixating on how stressful and difficult they are only intensifies your suffering by giving them power over you. Set a boundary for yourself to stop thinking about how troubling this person is, and focus instead on how you're going to go about handling their behavior in a positive way. This makes you more effective by putting you in the driver's seat, and it will greatly reduce the amount of stress you experience when you're interacting with them.

5. Maintain a level of emotional detachment from other people's opinions of you.

This one is vital for keeping stress at a distance. Not allowing negative people (or anyone, for that matter) to put the weight of their inadequacies on your back is vital to your emotional health and happiness. It all comes down to how you value yourself, and thus believe in yourself.

People who manage their lives effectively are generally those who work internally—those who know that success and well-being come from within (internal locus of control). Negative people generally work externally—blame others or outside events for everything that does or doesn't happen (external locus of control).

When your sense of satisfaction and self-worth are derived from the opinions of others, you are no longer in control of your own happiness. Know this. When emotionally strong people feel good about something they've done, they don't let anyone's shallow opinions or spiteful remarks take that away from them.

Truth be told, you're never as good as everyone says when you win, and you're never as terrible as they tell you when you lose. The important thing is what you've learned, and what you're doing with it.

6. Let go of the desire to change other people's negative tendencies.

Some people you can help by setting a good example; others you can't. Recognize the difference and it'll help maintain your equilibrium. Don't be taken in by the energy vampires, manipulators, and emotional blackmailers by desperately trying to control what is out of your control—other people's behavior.

For the most part, you can't change people, and you shouldn't try. Either you accept who they are and set a boundary or choose to live without them It might sound a bit harsh, but it's not. When you try to change people, they often resist and remain the same. But when you don't try to change them—and allow them the autonomy to be as they are—they often gradually change in the most miraculous way. Because what really changes is the way you see them.

7. Dedicate ample time every day to self-care.

You do not have to neglect yourself just because others do. Seriously, if you're forced to live or work with a negative person, then make sure you set boundaries in your schedule so that you get enough alone time to rest and recuperate. Having to play the role of a "focused, rational adult" in the face of persistent negativity can be exhausting, and if you're not careful, the negativity can consume you.

As mentioned previously, negative people can keep you up at night as you constantly question yourself:

- "Am I doing the right thing?"
- "Am I really so terrible that they speak to me like that?"

- "I can't *believe* he did that!"
- "I'm so hurt!"

Thoughts like these can keep you agonizing for weeks, months, or even years. Sadly, sometimes this is the goal of a negative person: to drive you crazy and bring you down to their level of thinking, so they're not wallowing alone. And since you can't control what they do, it's important to take care of yourself so that you can remain centered, feeling healthy and ready to live positively in the face of their negativity when you must.

Afterthoughts

Although it can be hard to admit, sometimes the negative person is ourselves. Yes, sometimes it's your own negativity that hurts you more than anything else.

If your inner critic is trying its hardest to get the best of you, try giving up all the thoughts and contemplations that make you feel bad, or even just some of them, for the rest of the day. See how doing that changes your life. You don't need these negative thoughts. All they have ever given you is a false self that suffers for no reason.

8 Things You Should Never Give Up for a Relationship

Being alone doesn't mean you're weak; it simply means you're strong enough to wait for the right relationship.

"IT'S BEEN EXACTLY ten years since my controlling, abusive ex-fiancé sold my favorite guitar, which cost almost a thousand dollars and took me ages to save for. He sold it on the day I broke up with him. When I went to pick up my belongings, he was proud that he had sold it to a local pawnshop. Luckily, I managed to track down the guy who bought it from the pawnshop. The guy was really sweet and gave it back to me for free, on the condition that I join him on his front porch for an hour and play guitar with him. He grabbed a second guitar, and we ended up sitting there on his porch for the rest of the afternoon, playing music, talking, and laughing. He's been my husband for almost nine years now, and we are happier than ever."

That's a paraphrased version of a story one of our coaching clients, Megan, lived through a while back. It's one of those life stories that really stuck with us—one that we still think about on a regular basis.

Using Megan's story as a frame of reference, we are reminded that unhealthy relationships restrict and impair, while healthy relationships bring freedom and life to our existence. It's important to remember the difference. It's important to remember what you should *never* have to give up for a relationship. And that's what this list is about—some good reminders about boundaries we need to uphold for ourselves:

1. Your imperfect magnificence

It's not hard to find someone who tells you they love you; it's hard to find someone who actually means it. But you will find them eventually, so don't rush love, and don't settle. Find someone who isn't afraid to admit they miss you. Someone who knows you're not perfect, but appreciates you as you are. One who gives their heart completely. Someone who says, "I love you," and then proves it day in and day out. Find someone who wouldn't mind waking up with you in the morning, seeing your wrinkles and gray hair, and then falling in love with you all over again.

Remember that, to the people who truly love you, you are magnificent already. This is not because they're blind to your shortcomings, but because they so vividly see the beauty of your soul. Your shortcomings then dim by comparison. The people who care about you are willing to let you be imperfect and magnificent, at the same time.

2. The right to decide for yourself

Don't put the only keys to your growth and happiness in someone else's pocket. Relationships are not about authority and obedience; they're agreements of love and respect. You simply can't live your entire life through someone else's fantasies. There must be compromise and the space to do what's right for you, even if someone you care about disagrees. Give, but don't allow yourself to be used. Listen to loved ones, but don't lose track of your inner voice in the process.

Never apologize for what you feel and what you don't feel; that's a betrayal of your truth. No matter how much advice people give you, sometimes you have to feel things out for yourself, make decisions on your own, experience things firsthand, and build your own conclusions from the ground up the old-fashion way.

3. Your innate human need to be understood

There's honestly nothing more intimate than simply being understood and understanding someone else in return. Even when there are disagreements, every healthy relationship contains this mutual understanding—a loving space filled with listening and compromise.

So remember to listen without defending, and speak without offending. Communication isn't just an important part of a relationship; it is the relationship. And really, there's only one rule for being a good communicator: the willingness to hear others. Because we do not always need a busy mind that speaks, just a patient heart that listens.

4. The freedom to love

Love is the creative force of the universe. It is as important to life as oxygen is to breathing. When it is present in our lives, we feel happier, more optimistic, and fulfilled. Without it, we become angry, cynical, resentful people, critical of ourselves and others, effectively squashing the greatness that exists in us and diminishing our own light.

Open your heart and let love out. Love people. Love experiences. Love yourself. And let go of those who try to stop you.

5. The courage and willingness to experiment with life

To live a great life, you must lose your fear of being wrong. Remember that doing something and getting it wrong is at least ten times more productive than doing nothing. Even when things don't work out, they do. Because in the end, experience is what you get when you didn't get exactly what you wanted, and experience is often the most valuable thing you have to give.

So don't be too timid and squeamish about your actions. Don't let someone scare you out of failing forward. All life is an experiment. The more experiments you make, the better. Either you will succeed or you will learn the next best step. Win-win.

6. Your joy

Never let anyone or anything get in the way of your joy. Live a life that sizzles and pops and makes you laugh out loud every day. Because you don't want to get to the end, or to tomorrow even, and realize that your life is a collection of meetings and "somedays" and errands and receipts and empty promises.

So go ahead and sing out loud in the car with the windows down, and dance in your living room, and stay up all night laughing, and paint your walls any color you want, and enjoy some port wine and chocolate cake. Yes, and go ahead and sleep in on clean white sheets, and throw parties, and paint, and write poetry, and read books so good they make you lose track of time. And just keep living and laughing and making God glad that He gave life to someone who loves and cherishes the gift.

7. Other important relationships, including the one you have with yourself

If a relationship is closing you off from the world, it's time to break free. It's time to choose love over deception. After all, that's what love is all about—freedom.

So don't blame love if a broken relationship is interfering with your other important relationships, or robbing you of your self-esteem and personal freedoms. No, don't blame love. For it isn't love that's stealing from you. It's possession. It's obsession. It's manipulation. It's confusion. Love has nothing to do with your situation. For love doesn't close the door on happiness and liberty. It opens it wide to let more in.

Likewise, if someone expects you to be someone you're not, take a step back. It's wiser to lose relationships over being who you are than to keep them intact by pretending to be someone else. It's easier to nurse a little heartache and meet someone new than it is to piece together your own shattered identity. It's easier to fill an empty space within your life where someone else used to be than it is to fill the empty space within yourself where *you* used to be.

8. Your inner peace and composure

No matter what you do or how amazing you are, throughout your lifetime some people will still upset you, disrespect you, and treat you poorly. Let them be; let karma deal with the cruel things they have done. Hatred and negativity filling your heart and mind will only consume you and your potential. You will begin to heal and grow emotionally when you let go of these past hurts, excuse the people who have wronged you, and forgive yourself for your misjudgments.

Bottom line: Learning to ignore certain people and situations is one of the great paths to inner peace. So let go when you must. Let them be, so you can be at peace.

9 Good Signs You're in the Right Relationship

It's not always where you are in life, but who you have by your side that matters.

"**HOW DO I** know if I'm in the right relationship or not?"

This is one of the most common questions our coaching clients ask us. And after we listen to the specifics of their situation, we often toss a question back at them to further clarify their thoughts and expectations. For instance:

"What do you think a 'right relationship' should provide for the people in it?"

Although the answer here is obviously subjective, in all relationships, romantic and platonic alike, there are some clear signs that things are going well. So let's take a look at some signs you're in the right relationship, along with corresponding tips that could potentially help you make a "wrong relationship" right:

1. No games are being played.

Far too often, we make our relationships harder than they have to be. The difficulties started when . . . conversations became texting, feelings became subliminal, sex became a game, the word "love" fell out of context, trust faded as honesty waned, insecurities became a way of living, jealously became a habit, being hurt started to feel natural, and running away from it all became our solution. Stop running! Face these issues, fix the problems, communicate, appreciate, forgive, and *love* the people in your life who deserve it. And, of course, if you feel like someone is playing games with you, speak up and establish some boundaries.

2. Everyone is on the same page.

If a woman starts out all casual with a man and she doesn't tell him that she wants a committed relationship, it will likely never become a committed relationship. If you give someone the impression that casual, or whatever, is okay with you, that's what will be assumed going forward. The bottom line is that you have to be straight from the start, or at least as soon as you know what you want. Don't beat around the bush. If someone gets scared and runs away because you were honest and set boundaries, that person wasn't right for you anyway.

3. The line of communication is open, honest, and clear.

It's better to talk and find out the truth than to keep going while silently wondering and get nowhere. Say what you mean and mean what you say. Don't expect the important people in your life to read your mind, and don't play foolish games with their heads and hearts. Don't tell half-truths and expect them to trust you when the full truth comes out—half-truths are no better than lies.

Listen without defending and speak without offending. Communication isn't just an important part of a relationship; it is the relationship. Relationships often fail because of trust issues, commitment issues, and, above all, communication issues. So be honest, commit, be clear about your expectations, and *communicate* always.

4. Loving deeds consistently reinforce loving words.

Nurture your important relationships so that when you tell the people you love that you love them, it's merely a ritualistic validation of what you have already shown them by how you treat them on a daily basis. Do little things every day to show your loved ones you care. Knowing that the person you're thinking of has you on their mind, too, means a lot.

Truth be told, you can say "sorry" a thousand times, or say "I love you" as much as you want, but if you're not going to prove that the things you say are true, they aren't. If you can't show it, your words are not sincere. It's as simple as that. And there's no such thing as a "right" relationship that isn't sincere at both ends.

5. Expectations of perfection are strictly forbidden.

Any relationship that's real will not be perfect, but if you're willing to work at it and open up, it could be everything you've ever dreamed of.

Your best friends and your soul mate may be far from perfect, but they are the right fit for you. Give them a chance to show you. When you stop expecting the people you love to be a certain way, you can start to enjoy and appreciate them for who they are. It's important to remember that every relationship has its problems, but what makes it perfect in the end is when you wouldn't want to be anywhere else, even when times are tough.

6. Honesty, vulnerability, and presence are held sacred.

Although it may sound risky, the strongest type of love is the one that makes you the most vulnerable. It's about daring to reveal yourself honestly, and daring to be open and transparent over the long term. It's about sticking by each other's side through thick and thin, and truly being there in the flesh and spirit when you're needed most.

So open yourself up. Truly be with the person you love. Allow yourself to experience them authentically. Tear down any emotional brick walls you have built around yourself and feel every exquisite emotion, both good and bad. This is real life. This is how you welcome a sincere connection with another human being.

7. There is a healthy blend of freedom and teamwork.

Keep in mind that we can't force anyone to be with us or love us. We shouldn't beg someone to stay when they want to leave. And likewise, we should never feel trapped in a relationship. In fact, if either person feels trapped, the relationship doesn't really exist. Because that's what relationships are all about: freedom.

Relationships are also built on a solid foundation of teamwork. And since relationships are one of the greatest vehicles of personal growth and happiness, the most important trip you will ever take in life is meeting someone else halfway. You will achieve far more by working with them rather than by working alone or against them. It really is a full circle. The strength of a relationship depends on the strength of its two members, and the strength of each member in the long run depends on the quality of the relationship.

And remember, relationships are rarely fifty-fifty at any given instant in time. You can't always feel 100 percent, or a full 50 percent of a relationship's whole—life is simply too unpredictable for that. So on the days when you can give only 20 percent, the other person must give 80 percent, and vice versa. It's never been about balancing steady in the middle; healthy relationships are about two people who are willing to make adjustments for each other in real time as needed, and give more when the other person can't help but give a little less.

8. Personal growth is embraced, celebrated, and shared.

It's not about finding someone to lose yourself in; it's about meeting someone to find yourself in. When you connect with someone special, a best friend or a lifelong partner, this person helps you find the best in yourself. In this way, neither of you actually meet the best in each other; you both grow into your best selves by spending time together and nurturing each other's growth.

When you honestly think about what you and your closest confidants add to each other's lives, you will often find that instead of giving or taking things from each other (advice, answers, material gifts, etc.), you have chosen rather to share in each other's joy and pain, and experience life together through good times and bad. No matter what, you two are there for each other, growing and learning as one.

9. Outsiders aren't calling the shots.

You have to live your own life your own way; that's all there is to it. Each of us has a unique fire in our heart for certain people. It's your duty, and yours alone, to decide if a relationship is right for you. You've got to stop caring so much about what everyone else wants for you and start actually living and deciding for yourself.

BOUNDARIES & EXPECTATIONS
QUESTIONS TO MAKE *YOU* THINK

What do you need to stop expecting from others?

What do people in healthy relationships *not* do?

What's one thing you will *not* let others do to you?

What helps you stay positive when negativity surrounds you?

What boundaries do you need to set to help protect yourself from negativity?

What should you *never* have to give up for a relationship?

In your experience, what are some good signs you're in the right relationship?

In what way do you need to start doing less?

How can you cultivate a better way of thinking and a calmer way of being?

In what area of your life do you need to loosen up and let go of control?

PART SEVEN

. . . . .

Love & Pain

Two Halves Don't Make a Whole

LOVE STARTS WITH you. Realize that two halves don't make a whole in a relationship. It takes two individual wholes who come together and create the magic of a relationship. When we have the belief that someone else is going to complete us, pain will develop as a result of that mistaken expectation.

You are a whole human being coming together with another whole human being, and then love is doing something for the other person. Pay close attention to them, figure out what their love language is, and channel that into demonstrating love to them in a way that they receive it. Be aware that what makes you happy and feeling loved will not always be the same for others. Paying attention more closely to the little things the other person desires that have nothing to do with you. You may notice things as simple as allowing the other person time to read a book, watch a football game, or just to be alone for a little while. Part of love is providing space for the other person to do the things they love.

How do you get there?

Start by answering the questions:

- What does love look like for you?
- How do you feel loved?

Share your answers with each other. By getting that question straight between two individuals in a relationship, you can avoid a lot of misunderstanding. Pain comes when that communication does not occur, when assumptions and expectations get the best of us. We enter a relationship with an expectation of how this person is supposed to behave, how they are supposed to love us, when we have never even communicated how we feel personally loved.

No matter how awkward it is, a conversation about how you feel loved will lay the groundwork for the relationship and allow for the understanding of each other's love language. Always keep that channel of communication open, because we evolve as people and need to have that conversation continually as we grow individually and together in a relationship.

Check in with each other on a regular basis. Sit down at the end of the day and share some quiet time together. It doesn't matter how you do it; what matters is that you make space to be still with each other with no agenda and see what arises between you. Otherwise pain can spiral out of control when you don't prioritize communicating and checking in with each other. You can't check in every four days, because emotions will build and problems will snowball.

To accomplish regular communication in our relationship, we leverage rituals that give us space for our daily check-in. We do things like going to the gym together every day, taking a weekly bike ride, trying something new every week, and visiting a new restaurant or movie theater.

Don't misinterpret this as us saying you need a date night every

Friday. No—we're saying to be intentional about creating space for your journey together. This can be fifteen minutes at the end of the day after everyone else is in bed. Before you turn on the TV, before you do the dishes, before you take a shower, sit down with your partner and check in with each other. It doesn't have to be a planned, extravagant, expensive event. It can be as simple as sitting at home in a quiet space, just the two of you, without doing anything.

7 Things to Remember When Someone You Love Is Depressed

THERE ARE WOUNDS that never show on our bodies that are deeper and more hurtful than anything that bleeds. Depression and heartbreak are two such wounds. We know from experience.

About a decade ago, in quick succession, we dealt with several significant back-to-back losses and life changes, including losing Angel's brother, Todd, to suicide; losing our mutual best friend, Josh, to cardiac arrest; and losing our home in the downturn of the economy. The pain inflicted by each of these experiences was absolutely brutal, and enduring them one after another broke our hearts and knocked us both into a moderate state of depression. There was a long stretch of time when we shut out the world, shut out each other, and avoided our loved ones, who were grieving alongside us.

Luckily, with the right support and the gradual restoration of our inner resolve, we pushed forward, stronger and with a greater respect for life. And while there were many intricate steps to our recovery process that we're leaving out here, the outcome of our journey ultimately led us to the work we do today, over a decade later. Through our course and coaching, we have spent the better part of the past ten years leveraging our lessons learned to guide amazing human beings through the process of coping with significant bouts of depression and heartbreak (and other forms of adversity). Though work has been anything but easy, it's also been incredibly rewarding and life-changing—it has undoubtedly been the most significant silver lining of the painful losses and life changes we were forced to endure.

In one of the radio interviews we did for our book, *Getting Back to Happy: Change Your Thoughts, Change Your Reality, and Turn Your Trials into Triumphs*, the talk show host asked the most sweeping question imaginable:

"What have you learned over the past ten years from coaching people through depression and heartbreak?"

We answered the question as best as we could, and tried to give decent insights within the time allotted. But we were off-air a minute or two later. So the truth is, we barely had enough time to graze the surface of such a complex and personal topic. But after that interview, we actually enjoyed thinking more deeply about it. In fact, we spent the entirety of our lunch break that day having a very open and candid conversation about what we have learned from both our own depression and heartbreak and the lessons that emerged afterward from coaching others through these painful states of mind. We took some notes while we chatted, and we'd like to share them with you.

While we are certain there's no "one size fits all" advice for depression and heartbreak, there are some very important general principles that apply to most people who are presently suffering. The reminders that follow, then, aren't universal clarifications, but simple guidelines that will hopefully give you a general starting point for supporting yourself or someone you love through the process of coping with depression and/or heartbreak.

1. Depression is not a state of mind you consciously or logically choose.

Being depressed is kind of like being lost deep in the woods. When you're lost deep in those woods, it might take you some time just to realize that you're lost. For a while, it's easy to convince yourself that you've just wandered off the path—that you'll find your way back any moment now. Then night falls, again and again, and you still have no idea where you are, and although it's agonizing to admit, you begin to realize that you've disoriented yourself so far off the beaten path, so deep into the thick of the woods, that you can't even tell which direction the sun rises or sets anymore. You're not choosing to be where you are, but you can't see a way out. That's how depression felt when we were struggling through it a decade ago.

Depression is one of the most helpless and tiring emotional experiences a person can live through. Sometimes it's feeling totally disoriented, sometimes it's feeling completely hopeless, and sometimes it's feeling absolutely nothing at all. There are times when depression can leave you feeling dead inside, incapable of moving and doing the things you used to enjoy. No one chooses to be depressed, and no one can turn it off or on in an instant whenever they feel like it. It's a state of mind that must be coped with and healed one tiny step at a time over the long term.

2. Depression is not simply a deeper state of heartbreak or sadness, and it's often misunderstood.

Heartbreak can be a trigger for depression, but depression is something altogether different. Depression isn't rational or emotional—it isn't a straightforward response to a tough situation. Depression just *is*, like rain in Seattle. It lingers, and it's hard to wrap your mind around if you haven't experienced it.

Some people may imply that they know what it's like to be depressed simply because they have gone through a divorce, lost a job, or lost a loved one. While these tough life situations can lead to depression, they don't create depression by default. In most cases these experiences carry with them strong emotional feelings (a key side effect of heartbreak). Depression, on the other hand, is often flat, hollow, and insufferable—literally sapping a person of emotion, hope, and reason.

You don't feel like *you*. You don't even feel human. You're disheartened and paranoid and humorless and lifeless and desperate and demanding, and no reassurance is ever enough. You're frightened, and you're frightening, and you're "not at all like yourself but will be better soon," but you know you won't.

Here's a chilling quote from *Infinite Jest*, by David Foster Wallace that brings this point home:

"The so-called 'psychotically depressed' person who tries to kill herself doesn't do so out of quote 'hopelessness' or any abstract conviction that life's assets and debits do not square. And surely not because death seems suddenly appealing. The person in whom 'its' invisible agony reaches a certain unendurable level will kill herself the same way a trapped person will eventually jump from the window of a burning high-rise.

"Make no mistake about people who leap from burning windows. Their terror of falling from a great height is still just as great as it would be for you or me standing speculatively at the same window just checking out the view; i.e. the fear of falling remains a constant. The variable here is the other terror, the fire's flames: when the flames get close enough, falling to death becomes the slightly less terrible of two terrors. It's not desiring the fall; it's terror of the flames. And yet nobody down on the sidewalk, looking up and yelling 'Don't!' and 'Hang on!', can understand the jump. Not really. You'd have to have personally been trapped and felt flames to really understand a terror way beyond falling."

3. Being loved when you are depressed feels like a massive burden.

"I don't want to see anyone. I lie in the bedroom with the curtains drawn and nothingness washing over me like a sluggish wave. Whatever is happening to me is my own fault. I have done something wrong, something so huge I can't even see it, something that's drowning me. I am inadequate and stupid, without worth. I might as well be dead."

That quote from Margaret Atwood's novel *Cat's Eye* reminds us of the desperate loneliness and isolation one feels when depressed. But even though depression makes you feel hopelessly alone, that's often exactly what depression motivates you to seek—more isolation. People suffering from depression typically feel like they're a burden on their loved ones. This causes them to isolate themselves and push away the very people they need.

So if someone you love becomes distant through their depression, just do your best to remind them as often as possible that you're still nearby, but don't force them to socialize or talk about their feelings if they don't want to. Be patient. Ease into it. Introduce plenty of small opportunities to create informal one-on-one time when you can break them out of their routine, even if it's just for a few minutes. Reach out to them at random intervals. Just be a present, living reminder that they are not alone.

4. Depression and heartbreak can exhaust the human spirit.

Relentless exhaustion is a common side effect of both depression and severe heartbreak. Just getting out of bed in the morning can be an overwhelming and excruciating experience. Also, someone suffering from these states of mind may feel okay one moment and then completely depleted the next, even if they're eating right and getting plenty of sleep. This can result in them canceling plans, departing get-togethers early, or saying no far more often than usual. These choices aren't personal attacks on friends and family—it has nothing to do with anyone else. These are just some of the prevalent side effects of working through severe mental anguish.

Again, if you love someone who is presently suffering, remind yourself that a human being can only give to others what they themselves have. Remind yourself that depression and, to a lesser degree, heartbreak, can take almost everything away. All your actions and words should come from a place of love, but that doesn't mean your depressed or heartbroken loved one will always be loving in return, and that's okay. When you do not take things personally, you liberate yourself—you open yourself to loving someone who truly needs you, freely, and without letting needless expectations get in the way of the immeasurable amounts of love you are capable of giving.

5. When you're depressed or heartbroken, the classic clichés never help.

"Time heals all wounds."

"It's not that big of a deal."

"You just need some fresh air."

"It's time to move on"

It's easy for people to say "positive" things like that with the best of intentions, but when you're suffering from depression or severe heartbreak, these kinds of clichéd phrases often come across the wrong way—thoughtless, empty, and essentially worthless.

In most cases, clichés like these don't address reality and only agitate the anxiety within, making a depressed or heartbroken person wish they were alone. It's like trying to strap a two-inch Band-Aid on a foot-long gaping wound.

So, if given the chance, what can you say instead? Again, there's no "one size fits all" answer. Just do your best to be sincere and supportive.

Here's a rough idea of what we might say (maybe not all at once):

"I love you, and I'm not the only one. Please believe me. Please believe that the people who love you are worth living for even when you don't feel it. Strive to revisit the good memories your depression (or heartbreak) is hiding from you, and project them into the present. Breathe. Be brave. Be here and take today just one tiny step at a time. Exercise because it's good for you, even if every step feels like it weighs nine hundred pounds. Eat when food itself sickens you. Reason with yourself when you have lost your reason. I'm here now, and I'll be here tomorrow too. I believe in you. We are in this together."

And then we'd give a long, silent hug.

6. Heartbreak can be a healthy anchor for healing and living well in the long run.

While depression disconnects us from our human emotions, and therefore must be carefully addressed, heartbreak by itself can actually help us move through our emotions. Heartbreak is never a pleasant experience, but it can be a healthy one when it's internalized in a healthy way. In fact, as human beings, we sometimes get used to the weight of our heartbreak and how it holds us in place. Angel once said, "My brother, Todd, will die over and over again for the rest of my life, and I'm okay with that. It keeps me closer to him." This was Angel's way of reminding us that heartbreak doesn't just break you down and disappear. Step by step, breath by breath, it becomes a part of you. And it can become a healthy part of you too—an anchor that keeps you grounded.

Truth be told, the wisest, most loving, and well-rounded people you have ever met are likely those who have been shattered by heartbreak. Yes, life creates the greatest humans by breaking them first. Their destruction into pieces allows them to be fine-tuned and reconstructed into a masterpiece. Truly, it's the painstaking journey of falling apart and coming back together that fills their hearts and minds with a level of compassion, understanding, and deep, loving wisdom that can't possibly be acquired any other way.

We have worked one-on-one with hundreds of these incredible people over the past decade, both online and offline, through various forms of coaching, side projects, and our live annual conferences. In many cases they came to us feeling stuck and lost, unaware of their own brilliance, blind to the fact that their struggles have strengthened them and given them a resilient upper hand in this crazy world. Honestly, many of these people are now our biggest heroes. Over the years they have given us as much as, if not more than, we have given them. And they continue to be our greatest source of inspiration on a daily basis.

7. Painful hardships often lead to post-traumatic growth.

To piggyback off the previous point, we want to briefly mention an emerging field of psychology called post-traumatic growth, which has proved that we, as human beings, are able to use various forms of hardships (including those that lead to severe heartbreak and even mild to moderate depression) for substantial intellectual development over the long term. Specifically, researchers have found that hardships can help us grow our contentment, emotional strength, and resourcefulness. When our view of the world as a safe place, or as a certain type of place, has been shattered, we are forced to reboot our perspective on things. With the right support and healing practices in place, we gradually gain the ability to see things with a fresh set of beginner's eyes again, which can be extremely beneficial to our personal growth.

Here is an excerpt on post-traumatic growth from our book *Getting Back to Happy*:

"We need to remember that all of us can heal through hardships, and many of us are even catapulted onto a more meaningful, motivated path after experiencing one. Growth through hard times is far more common than most of us realize. The challenge is to bring awareness to the opportunity presented by these kinds of unexpected and undesirable events. Afterward, we need hope. In the aftermath of intense pain, we need to know there is something better—and there almost always is. A traumatic experience is not simply a painful experience to be endured. Instead, it can be incredibly life changing by motivating us to evolve in the best ways possible.

"It isn't an easy journey, but most of us have the mental and emotional capacity to emerge from our hardships—even severe ones—stronger, more focused, and with a better perspective on life. In numerous psychological studies of people who have suffered traumatic hardships, about 50 percent of them report positive changes in their lives as a result of their negative experiences. Some changes are small (more appreciation for the average day, for example), while others are so seismic that they propel them onto totally new and rewarding life paths. The bottom line is that the most painful things that could possibly happen to us can be pivotal circumstances of great opportunity. Hardships often push us to face the reality of life's impermanence, to appreciate our limits, and to find more meaningful understandings of who we are and how we want to spend the rest of our lives."

5 Things to Remember When Someone You Love Loses Someone They Love

Tears shed for another person are not a sign of weakness; they are a sign of a pure, loving heart.

WE ALL KNOW deep down that life is short, and that death will happen to all of us eventually, and yet we are infinitely shocked when it happens to someone we love. It's like walking up a flight of stairs with a distracted mind and misjudging the final step. You expected there to be one more stair than there is, and so you find yourself off-balance for a moment, before your mind shifts back to the present moment and how the world really is.

We have dealt with the loss of siblings and best friends to illness, so we know from experience that when you lose someone you can't imagine living without, your heart breaks wide open. And the bad news is you never completely get over the loss—you will never forget them. However, in a backward way, this is also the good news.

You see, death is an ending, which is a necessary part of living. And even though endings like these often seem ugly, they are necessary for beauty too—otherwise it's impossible to appreciate someone or something, because they are unlimited. Limits illuminate beauty, and death is the definitive limit—a reminder that we need to be aware of this beautiful person, and appreciate this beautiful thing called life. Death is also a beginning, because while we have lost someone special, this ending, like the loss of any wonderful life situation, is a moment of reinvention. Although sad, their passing forces us to reinvent our lives, and in this reinvention is an opportunity to experience beauty in new, unseen ways and places. And finally, of course, death is an opportunity to celebrate a person's life and to be grateful for the beauty they showed us.

That's just a small slice of what coping with loss has taught us, and we're sure it has taught you some things as well. But, as we have recently been reminded, there's a big difference between understanding how to personally cope with loss and understanding how to help someone else cope with it. When someone you love and respect is grieving the loss of a loved one, the right words and gestures rarely come easy.

So the reminders below were for us as we attempted to comfort a dear friend who was grieving. These aren't universal clarifications, but simple guidelines that give us a general starting point for helping our grief-stricken loved ones cope and heal, gradually. Perhaps you will find value in them as well.

1. A person who's grieving already knows that time heals all wounds, and they don't need to be reminded of it.

When you're grieving, everyone wants to remind you that time will heal your pain, but no one can seem to tell you exactly what you're supposed to do and how you're supposed to cope right now. And that's all you really want to know.

Because it's right now that you can't sleep. It's right now that you can't eat. It's right now that you still hear his voice, and smell his scent, and sense his presence, even though you know he's not here anymore. It's right now that all you seem to be capable of doing is crying. So despite the fact that you intellectually know all about time's power to heal wounds, if you had all the time in the world right now, you still wouldn't know what to do with the immediate, intense pain you feel.

Realize this, and treat those who are grieving accordingly. Don't remind them that time heals. Instead, remind them that you're with them right now, and that you'll be available tomorrow too. Remind them that you love them and that you're standing beside them through their grief. Remind them that they aren't going through this alone.

2. Grief doesn't suddenly disappear, and some days are much better than others.

When someone you love passes away (or simply leaves), and you're not expecting it, you don't lose them all at once. You lose them a little bit at a time over weeks, months, and years—the way snail mail gradually stops coming to an address, and a person's scent slowly fades from the pillows and even from the clothes they used to wear.

Everyone grieves in their own way. For some of us, it could take longer or shorter. One thing you can be certain of, however, is that grief never completely disappears. An ember still smolders inside our grieving hearts, even when we've moved forward with our lives. Most days we don't notice it, but out of the blue it may flare to life. This reality is hard to deal with. We think we've accepted that they're gone—that we've grieved and it's over—and then *boom*! One little thing happens, and we feel like we've lost that person all over again.

This is exactly why caring for someone who's grieving requires incredible patience.

3. The grieving process exhausts and consumes a person, which is why you can't take their withdrawn behavior personally.

Relentless exhaustion is a common side effect of grief. Just getting out of bed in the morning can be an overwhelming and excruciating experience for a while. Also, someone suffering from grief may feel okay one moment and feel completely heartbroken the next, even if the environment around them hasn't changed one bit. This can result in them canceling plans, departing get-togethers early, or saying no far more often than you'd like. Just remember it's not about you—it has nothing to do with what you did or didn't do. These are just some of the prevalent side effects of working through the grieving process.

Do your best to not take anything they do personally. People can only give to others what they have, and deep grief takes almost everything away from a person. All your actions and words should come from a place of love, but that doesn't mean your grieving loved one will always be loving in return, and that's okay. When you do not take things personally, you liberate yourself—you open yourself to loving someone who truly needs you, generously, and without letting needless expectations get in the way of the immeasurable amounts of support and affection you are capable of giving.

4. A person who's grieving still wants to smile about the good times, and it's okay to help them reminisce.

In the long run, grief can devour us, or it can enlighten us. It depends on what we focus on. We can decide that a relationship was all for nothing if it had to end earlier than we expected, or we can recognize that every single moment of it had more meaning than we dared to accept at the time—so much meaning it frightened us, so we just lived, just took for granted the time spent together every day, and didn't allow ourselves to consider the sacredness of it.

When a wonderful relationship ends abruptly, we suddenly see what was there all along—it wasn't just a hug and a smile, not just a long walk together, not just meeting for lunch and talking about politics, people, and another day at work. It was *everything*—all the little intricacies of life shared by two souls. The answer to the mystery of living is the love and respect we share sometimes so imperfectly, and when the loss awakens us to the deeper beauty of it, to the sanctity of a wonderful relationship that's been lost, we're driven to our knees.

When this happens to someone you love—when they are mourning the loss of someone they love—help them focus on all those good, imperfect times worth smiling about. Help them counterbalance the weight of their loss with the weight of their gratitude for what preceded the loss.

5. Grief can be a burden, but also a healthy anchor for healing and living well.

As human beings, we sometimes get used to the weight of grief and how it holds us in place. Although we may never completely stop grieving, simply because we never stop loving the ones we've lost, we can effectively leverage our love for them in the present. We can love them and emulate them by living with their magnificence as our daily inspiration.

By doing this, they live on in the warmth of our broken hearts that don't fully heal back up, and we will continue to grow and experience life, even with our wounds. It's like badly breaking an ankle that never heals perfectly, and that still hurts when you dance, but you dance anyway with a slight limp, and this limp just adds to the depth of your performance and the authenticity of your character. Just knowing this and keeping it in mind can help us help our grieving loved ones dance again, gradually.

18 Things to Remember When Your Heart Is Breaking

IT'S A DULL, subdued sensation when your heart is breaking, like the muffled sound of a distant car crash. It doesn't physically pierce your skin or tear you to pieces, but the sensation is physically present—the paralyzing discomfort of realizing that something you took for granted is leaving for good.

Although it's hard to accept at first, this is actually a good sign, having a broken heart. It means you have loved something, you have tried for something, and you have let life teach you.

Life will attempt to break you down sometimes; nothing and no one can completely protect you from this reality. Remaining alone and hiding from the world won't either, for endless, stagnant solitude will also break you with unhealthy nostalgia and yearning.

You have to stand back up and put yourself out there again. Your heart is stronger than you realize. We've been there and we've seen heartbreak through to the other side. It takes time and patience.

Deep heartbreak is like being lost in the woods—every direction leads to nowhere at first. When you are standing in a forest of darkness, you cannot see any light that could ever lead you home. But if you wait for the sun to rise again, and listen when someone assures you that they themselves have stood in that same dark place and have since moved forward with their life, oftentimes this will bring the hope that's needed.

It's so hard to give you advice when you've got a broken heart, but some words can heal, and this is our attempt to give you hope. You are stronger than you know!

Please remember . . .

1. The genuine, loving emotion that breaks your heart is oftentimes the same emotion that will heal it, gradually, over time.

2. The person you liked or loved in the past, who treated you like dirt repeatedly, has nothing intellectually or spiritually to offer you in the present moment but more headaches and heartache.

3. You can mull it over and obsess and obsess about how things turned out—what you did wrong or should have done differently—but there's no point. It will *not* change anything right now!

4. Some chapters in our lives have to close without closure. There's no point in losing yourself by trying to hold on to what's not meant to stay.

5. Seven letters. Two words. One saying. It can either cut you open to the core and leave you in horrific pain, or it can free your heart and soul and lift an incredible weight off your shoulders. The saying: "It's over!"

6. When you don't get what you want, sometimes it's necessary preparation, and other times it's necessary protection. But the time is never wasted. It's a step on your journey.

7. Someday you're going look back on this time in your life as such an important time of grieving and growing. You will see that you were in mourning and your heart was breaking, but your life was changing.

8. Transitions in life are the perfect opportunity to let go of one situation to embrace something even better coming your way.

9. One of the hardest lessons to learn: You cannot change other people. Every interaction, rejection, and heartbreaking lesson is an opportunity to change yourself only.

10. Be determined to be positive. Understand that the greater part of your misery or unhappiness from this point forward is determined not by your circumstances, but by your attitude.

11. Life and God both have greater plans for you that don't involve crying at night or believing that you're broken. You aren't. You are growing!

12. It's always better to be alone than to be in bad company. And when you do decide to give someone a chance, do so because you're truly better off with this person. Don't do it just for the sake of not being alone.

13. When someone rejects you, it doesn't mean you need to also reject yourself or think of yourself as less worthy. It doesn't mean that nobody will ever want you anymore. Remember that there are billions of people in the world, and only *one* person has rejected you. And it only hurts so bad right now because, to you, that one person's opinion represented the opinion of the whole world. But that's not the truth.

14. Sometimes it takes a broken heart to shake you awake and help you see that you are worth so much more than you were settling for.

15. When you lose someone or something, don't think of it as a loss, but as a gift that lightens your load so you can better travel the path meant for you.

16. Most things that hurt you today only make you stronger in the end. They force you to grow.

17. When all is said and done, grief is the price you pay for love. And it's better to have loved, lost, and learned, than to have never loved at all.

18. A broken heart is just the growing pain necessary so that you can love more completely when the real thing comes along.

Afterthoughts

You are human and the human heart breaks sometimes. Don't fight it—fight through it! Give yourself a chance to love again, to feel again, and to live again.

You are alive and here to risk your heart by putting it into something you believe in, as many times as it takes. If you avoid taking this chance, one thing is certain: You will make it safely to the end, feeling empty and unfulfilled.

Don't do that to yourself.

You deserve better.

59 Short Love Stories to Cheer You Up

HERE'S A SELECTION of short love stories submitted to our sister site, Makes Me Think (MMT), that not only made us think, but warmed our hearts and cheered us up. We hope they do the same for you.

1. Today, my dad came home with roses for my mom and me. "What are these for?" I asked. He said that several of his coworkers were complaining about their wives and children today. He realized how lucky he was that after twenty years of marriage, and raising a daughter for the last seventeen years, he still had nothing to complain about.

2. Today, when I asked my grandfather for some relationship advice, he said, "Honestly, the moment I stopped trying to find the right woman and started trying to become the right man, your grandmother walked up to me and said, 'Hello.'" (Note: This was Marc's story.)

3. Today, it's been ten years since I told my best friend, Diego, that I wouldn't be able to attend the prom with him because my family was struggling to make ends meet and couldn't afford to buy me a ticket or a dress. Diego ended up buying me a dress and a ticket, and helping my

folks out with money by helping my dad, who had been unemployed for six months, find a good job. Ten years, a marriage, and one kid later, Diego still makes me think.

4. Today, on our fiftieth wedding anniversary, my husband took out an old envelope and handed me back the love note I wrote him in the seventh grade.

5. Today, it's been over ten years since I was a bag boy at a local grocery store. On Sunday mornings I held the front door open for our customers and greeted them. One particular older woman loved me for it. She actually told me on several occasions that one day I would make a lovely husband. This afternoon, I walked into that grocery store holding my wife's hand, and the same old woman was on her way out. She held the door for us, winked, and said, "I told you so."

6. Today, my wife and I sat down and watched the same movie at the same time. Despite being 9,000+ miles apart overseas on active duty, I felt like she was sitting right by me and I suddenly didn't feel so alone.

7. Today, it's been five years since I adopted a puppy from a high-kill shelter that had no time left. Since then I have developed a moderate case of a neurological disease that causes seizures. Believe it or not, the dog is able to detect my seizures before I do. She starts barking hysterically, and keys me into my episode before it starts. So today she is my service dog. The life I saved is saving me every day.

8. Today, it's been twenty-eight years since a firefighter saved my life when he rescued me from a burning condo building. In the process he suffered a leg injury that doctors said would leave him unable to walk

normally for life. This evening, he put down his cane and slowly walked our daughter down the aisle. My husband of twenty-seven years always makes me think.

9. Today, I finally stopped being foolish and called an old best friend I hadn't talked to in over a year. He single-handedly got me through one of the toughest times of my life, and in my depression I lashed out at him and dropped him from my life for selfish reasons. He answered the phone with: "Ready to pick up where we left off?" It instantly made me smile. Jason, you make me think.

10. Today was my little sister's fourteenth birthday. She has Down syndrome and doesn't have many friends. My boyfriend picked me up for dinner with flowers, but said they weren't for me. He came inside and handed them to my sister. She was so excited. He then took us both out to dinner to celebrate.

11. Today, I am a poor student, struggling to afford groceries and all the luxuries I was accustomed to. But every time I get a letter in the mail from my poppa telling me how much he loves me, or a phone call from my best friend just because she was thinking about me, I feel like the richest person in the world—in those moments I feel like I have everything I need.

12. Today, my mom and dad are recovering heroin addicts. They still go to their support groups, but both of them have been clean for seventeen years, since the day they found out my mom was pregnant with me.

13. Recently, my grandmother passed away. It was really hard on my entire family. She was the glue that kept our family together through

many hard times over the last decade. One of my close friends from college showed up at her ceremony. She paid her respects like everyone else, and gave me a huge hug before she left—a sincere hug that helped calm me inside. The interesting thing is, she never met my grandmother before, but she said she came today because, in her words, "Your grandmother is important to you, and you are important to me."

14. Today, my biological mother is deceased due to a drug overdose when I was only three years old. But today I can also proudly say I have the privilege of calling a beautiful woman, who has no blood relation to me, my mom. She is not my stepmom or official adopted parent. She is my best friend's mom who loves me enough to call me her daughter, and has for as long as I can remember.

15. Today, I got a phone call from my daughter's kindergarten teacher. She asked me why I wasn't providing lunch for my daughter over the past few days. Confused, I hung up the phone and asked my daughter what she was doing with her lunches. She said, "Katie's mom is in the hospital and hasn't been able to make any meals for the last week, so I gave a few of my lunches to her."

16. Today, after we all watched her blow out the ridiculous number of candles on her giant 100th birthday cake, my grandmother looked up at all twenty-seven of us—her children, grandchildren, great-grandchildren, and extended family—and said, "Look what I started. This family. I am so proud to be a part of your lives."

17. Today, it's been about two years since my ex-step-father tried to set my mom on fire, leaving her with burn scars on her face. Every week my little brother and I anonymously write a letter to her saying

how we think she's the most beautiful woman in the world (the truth), and we put it in the mailbox. She doesn't know it's us. But she cries when she opens them, and she just told us over dinner that the letters she's been receiving are helping her look up on days when she feels down.

18. Today, I helped make food for the homeless. The man I was giving the sandwich to said he didn't want it. I asked why and he pointed to his friend behind him and said, "I want the birthday boy here to have two sandwiches on his special day. It's the only gift I have to give." His friend was elated. People who have nothing and still give make me think.

19. Today, my best friend's new girlfriend, who he's had a crush on for a long time, finally admitted verbally that she "hates" me. He came up to me today, looking pretty upset, and told me what she said. And then he said, "So I broke up with her. Because if she doesn't respect you, she obviously doesn't respect me either."

20. Today, I walked past a woman walking two dogs. One dog was missing a leg, but they were both limping. I asked what happened. She smiled and explained that the injured dog had lost his leg in a dog fight before she adopted him, and that her other dog oftentimes "mimics him so he won't feel alone and different."

21. Today, after he finished giving his valedictorian commencement speech at his college graduation ceremony, he walked off the stage directly over to me, hugged me for a minute straight, and said, "Thank you for adopting me when I was five, and being the biggest inspiration a child could hope to have in a dad."

22. Today, while playing with my twenty-month-old daughter, I pretended to be sleeping. She covered me with a blanket, patted my back, then kissed me gently on the mouth—which is exactly what I do when I tuck her in at night. How closely our children watch us, and what they learn from our actions, makes me think.

23. Today, after my two-year-old daughter, who can't swim well, fell into our pool and began panicking, the stray dog I rescued from the pound last month jumped into the pool and pulled my daughter to the shallow steps . . . all in under ten seconds before I could make it from my lawn chair on the patio to edge of the pool.

24. Today, my baby sister wears her hair short, just like me. I'm fighting leukemia. My hair is short because of my chemo treatment. Her hair is short because, as she told my mom, "I want to be beautiful like my big sis."

25. Today, I waited at my boyfriend's house for half an hour before going home. As I angrily walked inside, I heard laughter. My clinically depressed brother, who hasn't cracked a smile in two months, was grinning as he watched a video on YouTube. Sitting next to him was my boyfriend holding the laptop. We had a miscommunication about where to meet, but when he saw my brother sitting alone, he decided to stay and keep him company. His kindness makes me think.

26. Today, at the nursing home I work at, I watched an elderly couple eat together as they do every day. They have been married sixty-three years. She had a stroke and can't stand, eat, talk, or do anything for herself. He doesn't need to live in a nursing home, but he does just to be

with her. Every day he eats his food, feeds her, and sits next to her, looking at her like he must have the day they were married. His unconditional, undying love and loyalty makes me think.

27. Today, he's driving to my college apartment to spend my last week of school with me. This will be the first night of the rest of our lives. After three years' dating long-distance, a twelve-month deployment to Iraq, and the rest of the time spent three states apart due to his serving in the Army, we are finally going to be together, permanently, in one place. Waiting this long for each other, and finally getting to start our life *together*, makes me happy and makes me think.

28. Today my ex-husband asked me to marry him. I said yes. We were married when I was nineteen, divorced later on, and then our lives somehow led our hearts back together. We are going to be married in two weeks, on what could have been our sixteenth wedding anniversary. Our children cried with joy when we told them today.

29. Today, when you dropped me off after we hung out, you called out to me as I stepped out of your car. You said, "Take care of yourself, okay?" and I responded with an absentminded, "Sure." But then your voice changed tone. "I'm serious, Jess. You're important to me. Take care of yourself," you repeated. You have no idea how much I needed that. Your true friendship makes me think.

30. Today, as I was sitting on the ledge of a cliff at a park, staring off into the distance and thinking, I turned around to see a girl almost in tears but trying to slowly walk down the ledge to where I was sitting. I got up and walked up to her and asked her what was wrong. She told me she

was deathly afraid of heights, but wanted to get over her fear because I looked lonely sitting by myself, and she wanted to make sure I was okay. Her braveness and kindness makes me think.

31. Today, it's been eight years to the day since he stopped doing drugs, cleaned up his act, and started caring for his younger siblings full-time. One of those siblings is me. When my parents died in a car accident eight years ago, my eighteen-year-old brother stepped up, got a job, and started taking care of me and my twin sister (who were both ten at the time) full-time. This evening my brother, who is now twenty-six, attended our high school graduation with a proud smile on his face.

32. Today, I broke down in front of my dad, frustrated with recently coming out to my family. I began to cry and yelled, "I'm sorry I'm gay!" He grabbed my tear-filled face and said sternly, "Don't ever apologize for who you are. Who you are is who I love. And who you are is beautiful."

33. Today, my father and I haven't spoken much in four years because apparently I just don't fit into his life. Earlier this week my stepdad called me worried sick because he missed my call and I'd left a voicemail while I was crying. He was ready to drive a couple hours to my school if something had happened. His caring, and the fact that my mom found a man who loves me like his real daughter, makes me think.

34. Today, after years of struggling with my weight, and dealing with an overweight family in denial, my children ages five and seven rode their bikes and ran with me while I worked out. My wife started working out

too. My kids are super excited about their upcoming races with me and their mom. Realizing that the things I do and say matter, and that we're all in this together as a family, makes me think.

35. Today, my mother had my grandfather—my father's father—over for Easter Sunday dinner because his wife passed away and my dad was away on business. My mom and dad have been divorced for thirteen years, but my mom didn't want my grandfather to be alone. Her kindness makes me think.

36. Today, I was behind a bigger guy and his wife in line for a roller coaster. They seemed to have come with a big group of people, but I could tell he was nervous. When he fit it into the cart, tears rolled down his cheeks and the entire group started cheering. It turns out he just lost a hundred pounds and hasn't been able to ride a roller coaster for twelve years. Every person around him was his friend, and they were there to support him.

37. Today, I was stressing out over school and work, along with a lot of personal problems that have popped up in my life lately. In the middle of the stress, I received an email from a woman I regularly babysit for. She told me that her little daughter I babysit cut out my picture from a news article I was in and taped it to her bedroom wall. Knowing that I matter that much to her made me smile, even today.

38. Today, I waited on an elderly couple where I work. She kept forgetting things. Turns out she has Alzheimer's disease. Her husband was so calm and understanding. He never got annoyed having to tell her everything she had forgotten. I witnessed true love at its best.

39. Today my best friend, who has been my best friend for over ten years, confessed that he used to be depressed in high school. I felt like a horrible friend and asked out loud how I never picked up on it. He looked at me, laughed, and said, "You probably never picked up on it because I couldn't help but smile when I was around you. You're the reason I made it through."

40. Today, I came across my mom's old journal in the attic. I read a few entries, and they were quite depressing. My mom has always been such a positive influence in my life, so I had no idea her past was so troubled. The final entry was written the day before I was born. I told my mom I found her journal and asked her why she stopped keeping a journal after I was born. She said, "I found happiness. I finally had something amazing to live for."

41. Today, as my eighty-one-year-old mother and I sat in the waiting area of a restaurant, the 1960s song "Don't Worry Baby" by the Beach Boys came on the radio, and she started to smile. "What are you smiling about?" I asked. "This was our song—your dad and I, that is," she said. "You know, your dad has been gone for almost a decade, and it's been nearly fifty years since he and I first heard this song playing in a nightclub. But every time I hear it, it reminds me of that night, dancing with him on our first official date. And that makes me smile."

42. Today, in a little African village where I volunteer as a nurse, I passed out food to hungry children. And since I knew her only food for the day was the slice of wheat bread I had just given her, I did not let her see me cry when she tore the slice in two and gave the bigger half to her little brother.

43. Today, it's been a year since I won my court case. Fourteen months ago my neighbor was abusing his dog. So I stole the dog, got arrested, fought a two-month legal battle with every cent I had, and won. And now every night when the dog jumps in bed with me, I know it was worth it.

44. Today, my dad handed me a bottle of Windex and a roll of paper towels as we got in the car. He turned to me and said, "I just talked to your mom while she was on her lunch break. She mentioned her windshield got covered in bugs on the drive to work. Since we're going to drive right by her work anyway, I figured we'd clean them off for her. It's the little things, kiddo, which keeps love going." By chance, while my dad was cleaning the windshield, my mom came out with her kids for recess. Her smile and seeing how in love my parents are makes me think.

45. Today, it's been five years since I was severely beaten by three bullies at a college party for stopping them from trying to bring a drugged girl home with them. I lost a tooth and received two black eyes and severely bruised ribs from the incident, but I stopped them. This girl was my crush for three years but had never noticed me as boyfriend material until that night. When I woke up in ICU twelve hours after I was beaten up, she was sitting beside my bed, asleep while holding my hand. Since then, we've been steadily dating for five years and are engaged to be married. Who says nice guys finish last?

46. Today, I received this text message from my fiancé: "I want this too. I want all of it. I want the pointless bickering, the long walks, the late-night phone calls, the good-morning texts. I want cute pictures with you, to hold your hand, to make food for you, to call you baby. The

joking, the wrestling, the fights, the long 'how I feel' text messages on the days we aren't on the same page. I want to be one of those inseparable best-friend couples that people are like 'you're still together?' That's what I want. With you."

47. Today, as she laid in her hospital bed, just before my grandmother took her last breath, she smiled and said, "Hello, Charles." Charles was my grandfather's name. He died in 1998.

48. Today, on our ten-year wedding anniversary, my middle school/high school sweetheart wrote me a love letter for the very first time. The final sentence reads, "I love you more every day, and I'm so proud to say we've been inseparable since we were dinosaurs wreaking havoc on the playground so many moons ago."

49. Today, four years after I lost my hearing after making a full recovery from meningitis, my boyfriend of seven years asked me the four-word question every girl wants to hear. But I never imagined how perfect it would look as it did when he signed it to me.

50. Today, I was feeling very down while heading out to a family dinner. I was in the back seat of the car with my twelve-year-old brother, who's never affectionate to me. My boyfriend had just dumped me, but I didn't want to tell my family yet. While I sat in the car with my sunglasses on to cover my tear-filled eyes, my little brother looked at me a few times and then reached over and held my hand for the rest of the car ride.

51. Today, after dreaming about it for the last ten years, she sat down on my lap in my wheelchair with me and kissed me on the lips. And then she paused for a second, smiled, and went in for another.

52. Today, after spending nearly twenty-four years of my life self-conscious of being a six-foot-two woman, and being taller than most of the guys, I fell in love and married a guy in a wheelchair.

53. Today, after nearly twelve years without an intelligible word spoken, my deaf daughter hugged me tight and said, "I love my daddy!"

54. Today, I accidentally sent a text message intended for my husband to my father-in-law. Luckily it only said "I love you." My father-in-law sent me a really sweet reply and signed it "Love, Dad" for the first time since we've been family.

55. Today, I work at a high school as guidance counselor, and today was "Music Genre Day." The principal and administrative staff encouraged teachers and students to dress (appropriately) in a way that symbolizes their favorite musical style. I dressed in the grunge style (a flannel shirt, jeans, and messy hair), much like I did in middle and high school. After work I stopped by the nursing home to see my grandmother, who has Alzheimer's. And for the first time in almost two years, she recognized me! She said, "My sweet Katie!" as soon as she saw me.

56. Today, I was in Central Park trying to write a new chapter in my novel. The writing was going at a snail's pace—I just couldn't seem to type the right words. And I began to get frustrated and depressed. Then out of left field, an attractive woman sitting on a bench across the path from me got up, walked over to me, smiled, placed a paper on my table, and left without a word. It was a gorgeous sketch of me thinking and writing. I instantly smiled and wrote the rest of the chapter with a grin. And when I was done writing, I realized her name and phone number were written on the backside of the sketch.

57. Today, it's been two years since my mom lost her battle with cancer. She was forty at the time, and I was thirteen. Since then her best friend, Joy, has treated me like her own daughter. She picks me up for school three days a week on the mornings my dad has to leave early, packs me lunches, takes me to doctor's appointments, talks to me about the birds and the bees, etc. Recently I told her that I appreciate it, and she replied, "There's no reason to thank me. As far as friends go, your mom was my soul mate. And although I decided to never have kids, I have one, you. I love you like my own daughter."

58. Today, it's been a couple weeks since I got unexpectedly laid off two days before Christmas. Unemployment only pays me about 20 percent of what I've been making for the last five years. I had to move from a 1,500-square-foot apartment into a 400-square-foot studio to make ends meet. I've been really stressed out for many reasons, but mainly because my fiancé comes from a pretty wealthy family. I sometimes worry I don't financially live up to her expectations. Tonight, she came to see me when she got off work. We were sitting on the couch, and I asked her if she was comfortable. She immediately snuggled her head into my chest and said, "This, right here, always feels like home."

59. Today, it's been exactly six months since I took on the responsibility of caring for my seventeen-year-old severely autistic brother. He rarely talks and prefers to be alone. Today while I served him his favorite meal for dinner, he gave me a huge hug out of the blue and said, "Thank you, my beautiful big sister!" His gesture made me cry from joy and certainly makes me think.

One Popular Love Story That Breaks Too Many Hearts

IT'S TIME TO let go of the heartbreaking cultural story—or fairy tale—of "happily ever after."

Our always-in-your-face, airbrushed media culture—with its continuous stream of picture-perfect highlight reels—has built the expectation in us that life is supposed to be like an endless day at Disney World. And nowhere does our media culture present a more skewed set of expectations than around our relationships. We are swayed to believe a great relationship is all sunshine and roses, despite the fact that most of us have witnessed firsthand plenty of examples to the contrary.

It's time to get our heads wrapped around this once and for all!

Human relationships require effort and compromise. They require two people to practice patience and presence and thoughtfully extend themselves for the sake of the other. They require us to redefine the fairy-tale story of love that our media culture has attempted to brainwash us with.

It's time to take a stand and acknowledge the fact that we've been fed lies most of our lives. **We've been told that love is a feeling worth** finding, but the reality is that love is an action worth investing in. It's something two people must commit to as a daily ritual.

When you're able to accept this new reality, and get past the fantasy about things needing to be magical all the time, you make room for the real joy of engaging deeply in a real relationship, which holds a powerful, flexible space that widens itself to accommodate the necessary struggles.

Let this sink in right now . . .

When your marriage, friendship, parenting, etc., get difficult, it's not an immediate sign that you're doing it wrong. These intimate, intricate relationships are toughest when you're doing them right— when you're dedicating time, having the tough conversations, and making sacrifices for each other.

Again, there is no soul mate, best friend, or family member out there who will solve all your problems. There is no love at first sight that lasts without work and commitment. But there are, of course, people out there worth fighting for. Not because it's easy, but because they're worth it. Not because they're perfect, but because they're imperfect in all the ways that are right for you. You challenge each other's thinking and behavior, but also support each other's ability to change and grow. You complement each other's flaws in a way that allows your souls to unite and operate more efficiently as one over the long run.

The awareness of all this, as you know, is often incredibly hard to come by. Especially in the beginning. And to that end, let us share (with permission) a quick true story with you about one of our newest course students:

What We Have Been Searching for All Along

About a decade ago, on his thirty-seventh birthday, after spending his entire adult life loosely dating different women, he finally decided he was ready to settle down. He wanted to find a real mate . . . a lover . . . a life partner—someone who could show him what it meant to be in a deep, monogamous, trusting relationship.

So he searched far and wide. There were so many women to choose from, all with great qualities, but none with everything he was looking for. And then, finally, just when he thought he would never find her, he found her. And she was perfect. She had everything he ever wanted in a woman. And he rejoiced, for he knew how rare a find she was. "I've done my research," he told her. "You are the one for me."

But as the days and weeks turned into months and years, he started to realize that she was far from perfect. She had issues with trust and self-confidence, she liked to be silly when he wanted to be serious, and she was much messier than he was. And he started to have doubts . . . doubts about her, doubts about himself, doubts about everything.

And to validate these doubts, he subconsciously tested her. He constantly looked around their apartment for things that weren't clean just to prove that she was messy. He decided to go out alone to parties with his single guy friends just to prove that she had trust issues. He set her up and waited for her to do something silly just to prove she couldn't be serious. It went on like this for a while.

As the tests continued—and as she, clearly shaken and confused, failed more and more often—he became more and more convinced that she was not a perfect fit for him after all. Because he had dated women in the past who were more mature, more confident, and more willing to have serious conversations.

Inevitably, he found himself at a crossroads. Should he continue to be in a relationship with a woman he once thought was perfect but now realizes lacks the qualities that he'd already found in the other women that came before her? Or should he return to the lifestyle he had come from, drifting from one empty relationship to the next?

After he enrolled in our Getting Back to Happy course, desperately looking for answers, this is the gist of what we told him:

One of the greatest lessons we learn in life is that we are often attracted to a bright light in another person. Initially, this light is all we see. It's so bright and beautiful. But after a while, as our eyes adjust, we notice this light is accompanied by a shadow . . . and oftentimes a fairly large one.

When we see this shadow, we have two choices: We can either shine our own light on the shadow, or we can run from it and continue searching for a shadowless light.

If we decide to run from the shadow, we must also run from the light that created it. And we soon find out that our light is the only light illuminating the space around us. Then, at some point, as we look closer at our own light, we notice something out of the ordinary. Our light is casting a shadow too. And our shadow is bigger and darker than some of the other shadows we've seen.

If, on the other hand, instead of running from the shadow, we decide to walk toward it, something amazing happens. We inadvertently cast our own light on the shadow, and likewise, the light that created this shadow casts its light on ours. Gradually, both shadows begin to disappear. Not completely, of course, but every part of the two shadows that are touched by the other person's light illuminate and disappear.

And as a result, we each find more of that bright beautiful light in the other person.

Which is precisely what we have been searching for all along.

Time to Practice

Let's consciously remind ourselves, again and again, that **there is no shadowless light.**

Let's embrace the fact that the deepest craving of human nature is the need to be appreciated as is, and that too often we try to be sculptors, constantly carving out of others the image of what we want them to be—what we think we need, love, or desire. But these actions and perceptions are against reality, against their benefit and ours, and always end in disappointment.

So, today . . .

- **Instead of looking for more signs of what's not working in your relationships, look for signs of what is.** Because, as you know, what we focus on grows stronger in our lives.
- **Instead of trying to change others, give them your support and lead by example.** If there's a specific behavior someone you love has that you're hoping disappears over time, it probably won't. If you absolutely need them to change something, be honest and put all the cards on the table so this person knows what you need and why.
- **Instead of getting frustrated and tuning out, tune in.** Remember, when you tune out and disengage in any way, you are engaging in the silent treatment. And all variations of the silent treatment don't just remove the other person from the disagreement you're having with them; they end up removing them, emotionally, from the relationship or conversation you're having with them, and the understanding you hope to reach. When you're ignoring someone, you're really teaching them to live without you. So tune yourself back in!
- **Instead of looking for "easier," appreciate the sacrifices.** Remind yourself of what a healthy long-term relationship is: a practice where

two people wake up every morning and say, "This is worth it. You are worth it. I am happy you are in my life." It's about sacrifice. It's about knowing that some days you will have to do things you dislike to make the one you love smile, and feeling perfectly delighted to do so.

And yes, love is a practice. **A daily rehearsal of honesty, presence, communication, acceptance, forgiveness, sacrifice, and stretching the heart and mind through new and vulnerable dimensions.** Let's practice together. Today.

The Unwritten Love Poem: Why True Love Is So Hard to Express

TO END THIS section on love and pain, we want share a love story that Marc wrote:

Twenty years ago, I wrote an unsigned love poem to a girl I barely knew. I told Brianna, among other things, that life was a blaze of magnificence, that she made it even brighter, and that someday I would spend every day with the prettiest girl in the world.

When she read the poem she got goose bumps, smiled from ear to ear, and daydreamed about the gentleman behind the poetic prose. She showed it to her sister, who sighed and said, "How romantic! I wish someone would write me a poem like that." Then she showed it to her parents. Her mom smirked, but her dad frowned and said, "Don't waste your time on a foolish boy hiding behind a silly poem." Finally, she let her new boyfriend read it. In a grim voice he said, "Let me know when you find out who wrote it, because I'd like to give him a piece of my mind!"

Despite reactions ranging from enthusiasm to aggravation, she kept the poem and still has it in her possession today, two decades later. Her younger brother, Jose, recently found it neatly folded and tucked between two pages of an old photo album she keeps in her den.

I know all of this because Jose told me. He and I met in school twenty years ago, and we have been best friends ever since. He was, frankly, the reason I wrote the poem.

A Second Glance

"Your sister is pretty," I told Jose during my first visit to his home.

"Forget about it," he said. "Brianna has buff guys fighting for her affection every day. You couldn't hold her attention long enough to get a second glance."

"I could if I wrote her a poem," I replied.

"She has guys writing her romantic crap all the time," he said. "She'll just toss it out with all the other failed attempts."

"Not mine," I insisted.

"You're crazy." He chuckled. "Go ahead and try. Make me laugh!"

I wrote the poem that evening and mailed it anonymously the next morning.

"I Thought I Was Special"

The poem I wrote Brianna wasn't genuine, at least not in my mind. I wrote it because Jose doubted me. Sure, I thought Brianna was pretty, but I didn't want to have a serious relationship with her. At the time, I didn't even know her. And as it turns out, she and I have almost nothing in common.

The last genuine love poem I wrote went to a girl I met a month before I met Brianna. She was on the varsity soccer team, and her beauty was majestic. I wrote Sara a poem and slipped it into her locker the same afternoon. I confessed my desire to be a soccer ball and risk being kicked around, if it was the only way I could catch her attention. She caught up with me the next morning and told me I didn't need to transform into a soccer ball to catch her attention. I asked her out on a date a few minutes later.

Our first date went well. But the next afternoon, Sara spoke to a few of her teammates, two of whom I had previously dated. She was appalled when she found out that I had written Jackie a poem about innocent kisses blown her way in the breeze, and Carol a poem about the lucky sunshine that glistens off her skin. Needless to say, a second date was not in our future.

"Stupid me! When I read the poem you wrote me, I actually believed you were being sincere! I thought I was special!" Sara screamed.

"I was . . . and you are," I mumbled as she stomped away.

But Sara had a point. Although I had never summoned the desire to be a soccer ball in any of my previous poems, I did use similar analogies that carried the same fundamental message of flirtatious affection.

I wasn't trying to hurt her. I thought she was gorgeous. I thought she carried herself with amazing grace. I wanted to be around her. I wanted to be hers. She was the most perfect girl in the entire world . . . and I'd felt this way a hundred times before.

No Two Words Would Rhyme

Roughly six months after I met Brianna, I met Angel. I realized shortly thereafter that she moved me in a way the others had not. I couldn't consciously pinpoint it, but I knew our relationship felt special. Even after the initial excitement waned, she kept me captivated. I was wide awake in the second inning for the first time in my life.

Angel and I have been together for nineteen years now—we've been through a lot together—and I appreciate her more and more with each passing day. Yet despite my love for her, she's never received a love poem.

It's not that I haven't tried. I tried, once, to write her a poem about the depth and beauty of her hazel-green eyes. I stumbled over my words. Another time I tried to write her a poem about the mornings I wake up early just to watch her sleep. I failed again. And just last month I tried to write her a poem titled "Amidst an Angel." But no two words would rhyme.

Nineteen years and not a single love poem written. Of course, Angel knows I love to write, so she has occasionally questioned my motives for never writing her a romantic piece.

Yesterday evening I found myself trying again. I tried to poetically re-create the story of our first encounter. I wanted to make it cute. I wanted to make her smile. I wanted to make her cry tears of joy. I wanted to typify our tale in exquisite prose. Nothing came.

"The Most Profound Affirmation"

I fell asleep around midnight last night thinking about my predicament. Have I completely lost my touch? Has someone cast an evil spell on me? Or is there a more profound, philosophical explanation?

Zzzz . . .

I dreamed I was sitting at a round table in a dimly lit room. There was a man sitting across the table from me. He looked a lot like me, only his hair was silver and his skin was worn.

"I'm here to answer your question," he said.

"What question?" I asked.

"The one you've been asking yourself for almost two decades," he replied.

"What's wrong with me?" I huffed. "Why can't I write Angel a love poem?"

"Perhaps you can't write her a love poem because you realize, subconsciously, that leaving it unwritten is the most profound affirmation of love you can make. Because you truly do love her, and true love cannot be translated into words. Because words alone could never do her any justice."

I nodded in agreement.

He went on, "The sad truth, of course, is that this affirmation of true love will always remain unnoticed. Because there is no visible output to notice—no poem to read."

My eyes popped open.

Inspired to Write

It was 4:30 a.m., but I was wide awake and inspired to write about the epiphany I had in my dreams. I leaned over, kissed Angel on the forehead, and rolled out of bed. I powered on my laptop. After gazing at the blank white screen for several minutes, I placed my fingers on the keyboard and titled the page:

"The Unwritten Love Poem: Why True Love Is So Hard to Express."

Afterthoughts

Why did I just share that story with you?

Because doing so helps remind me.

And I know you need a reminder sometimes too.

Sometimes we all need to be reminded of the beauty and sweetness of truly loving someone without the forced glitz, glam, and airbrushing of the Instagramming world we live in. Because it's so easy to forget. It's so easy to see the fairy-tale highlight reel of staged romance that scrolls across our screens and feel inadequate in comparison.

We need to remind ourselves that loving someone—truly and profoundly loving them—isn't about crafting the perfect love poem, photographing the perfect internet kiss, or showing off in any way; it's about showing up every day behind closed doors to quietly respect and support someone who means the world to us.

LOVE & PAIN QUESTIONS
TO MAKE *YOU* THINK

Do you have personal experience with depression or heartbreak?

Have you ever helped a loved one cope with either?

How has judging people affected you and your relationships?

What is your short love story that makes you smile?

What relationship truths have you learned that have helped your relationships thrive?

When you think about real love, how do you describe one thing it never does to you?

Have you been making sure the people you spend time with are good, kind, and honest?

Which of your important relationships deserve a little more of your time and attention?

Who is draining the energy and spirit out of your soul (that you need to let go of)?

When is the last time you took time to offer value to someone who needed it?

Final Note

WHETHER YOU CALL it a squad, a network, a tribe, or a family—whoever you are, you need one. You need a small group of people in your life who lift you higher.

As Anaïs Nin so profoundly observed, "Each friend represents a world in us, a world possibly not born until they arrive, and it is only by this meeting that a new world is born."

So right here, right now, make it a goal to spend more time with nice people who are smart, driven, and like-minded. Remember that relationships should help you, not hurt you. Surround yourself with people who reflect the person you want to be. Choose friends you are proud to know, people you admire, who love and respect you—people who make your day a little brighter simply by being in it.

Ultimately, the people in your life make all the difference in the person *you* are capable of being and the impact you're able to have on others.

If You Want to Continue Your Journey with Us

THE GETTING BACK TO HAPPY course is an online, self-paced course designed to help you take what you've learned in this book to the next level, with included one-on-one (and two-on-one) coaching directly from us.

Getting Back to Happy is the go-to course for anyone serious about taking action to reclaim their happiness and realize their potential. It will help you wake up every day and live with a fuller sense of purpose, even if you've tried everything else. If you've been wanting a way to work with us, this is it. It's the result of more than a decade of study and one-on-one coaching with hundreds of people just like you from all over the world. It's a proven system that works time and again to bust people out of their ruts and get them back on track to living a life they are excited about. From proven ways to foster stronger relationships to actions engineered to help you let go of painful emotions, the learning modules in this course will inspire and equip you to become your best self.

When you enroll in Getting Back to Happy, you'll receive access to a massive collection of helpful resources. From inspiring stories to actionable strategies to lots of live-engagement opportunities (phone calls and video calls) with us, Getting Back to Happy provides more than just great content: It fosters an uplifting community. Everyone who enrolls in Getting Back to Happy will get lifetime access to a supportive community and self-paced online course that's packed with sixty HD video trainings, including hundreds of scientifically proven methods for getting back on track, and members-only discussion forums where you can discuss each lesson with both of us and other course members.

LEARN MORE ABOUT Getting Back to Happy and enroll at marcandangel .com/getting-back-to-happy.

THE THINK BETTER, Live Better live conference is the go-to event for you if you're serious about taking action to reclaim your happiness and realize your true potential. Think Better, Live Better is designed to help you wake up every day and live life with a full sense of purpose, even if you've tried everything else. If you want to attend a life-changing conference filled with world-class personal development experts who care, this is it!

Think Better, Live Better is packed full of practical strategies and unforgettably inspiring lessons for living a more positive and productive life. But this is more than just an event. It's an immersive experience that will give you proven tools to identify and transform the negative, self-limiting beliefs and behaviors that keep you stuck. From proven ways to foster healthier relationships, to actions engineered to help you let go of painful experiences and emotions, to rituals guaranteed to increase your productivity, the actionable talks and workshops at this event—delivered by some of the brightest minds in personal growth—will inspire and equip you to become your most effective self.

This event is your gateway to the life you've planned on living. You won't leave Think Better, Live Better with a notebook full of ideas and nothing checked off your to-do list. Instead, you'll set into motion a realistic plan you can keep improving on for years to come. We will guide you step-by-step through mental-strength exercises, and help you refocus your mind on the powerful truths that will have the fastest and most effective impact on your personal and professional desires and goals.

Learn more and register for the next event at thinklivebetter.com.

Think Better, Live Better **podcast**. You can't control what happens to you every moment. But you can absolutely control how you respond to the challenges of each and every day. Marc and Angel lead us through relevant and helpful topics about self-improvement, time management, relationships, family, motivation, and discipline. Their thoughtful, insightful, and conversational style is not only enjoyable and memorable but also eminently practical. Think better and begin to live better today. You can listen to the newest episodes on your favorite podcast player right now by searching for *Think Better, Live Better* on Apple iTunes, Spotify, or Google Podcasts.

About the Authors

Passionate writers, admirers of the human spirit, and full-time students of life, Marc and Angel Chernoff enjoy sharing inspirational advice and practical tips for life on their popular personal development blog, *Marc and Angel Hack Life*. Currently the site contains about six hundred articles on productivity, happiness, love, work, and general self-improvement, and has attracted seventy million page views since its inception in summer 2006. They are authors of the *New York Times* bestseller *Getting Back to Happy*.

Marc and Angel both share a great passion for inspiring others to live to their fullest potential, and they honestly feel best when they are inspiring others to be their best. They started their blog with the goal of inspiring as many people as possible. And they work passionately every day to fulfill this goal through the thoughts and ideas they share online.

Please catch up with them at www.marcandangel.com.

Or you can email them: angel@marcandangel.com and marc@marcandangel.com.

Subscribe for Free

If you have enjoyed this book and found it useful, you will love all the other articles at *Marc and Angel Hack Life*. Readers continually leave feedback on how they have benefited tremendously from the site's material and how it's a staple for their personal growth.

By **subscribing**, you will receive free practical tips and inspirational advice geared for productive living, served fresh three times a week directly to your in-box: marcandangel.com/subscribe.

LET'S CONNECT

We would love to hear from you and to know what you think. Feel free to get in touch with us via the following channels:

Facebook.com/marcandangelhacklife
Twitter.com/marcandangel
Instagram.com/marcandangel

Also by Marc and Angel Chernoff

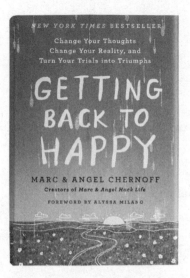

Empowering advice for overcoming setbacks and bouncing back from tough times. A *New York Times* bestseller.

Powerful advice and instant inspiration for becoming our best selves.

tarcher
perigee